To Mrs. Pudek (aka Sue),
for teaching me poetry is a superpower too.—T.S.

To every small and powerful reader.—A.S.

23 24 25 26 27 5 4 3 2 1

Greystone Kids / Greystone Books Ltd.
greystonebooks.com

Cataloguing data available from Library and Archives Canada
ISBN 978-1-77164-656-7 (cloth)
ISBN 978-1-77164-657-4 (epub)

Editing by Kallie George
Copy editing and proofreading by Becky Noelle
Jacket and interior design by Sara Gillingham Studio
The illustrations in this book were rendered with Photoshop and a magnifying glass.

Printed and bound in China on FSC® certified paper at Shenzhen Reliance Printing.
The FSC® label means that materials used for the product have been responsibly sourced.

Greystone Books thanks the Canada Council for the Arts, the British Columbia Arts Council, the Province of British Columbia through the Book Publishing Tax Credit, and the Government of Canada for supporting our publishing activities.

Canada

British Columbia | British Columbia Arts Council
An agency of the Province of British Columbia

Canada Council for the Arts | Conseil des arts du Canada

FSC www.fsc.org MIX Paper from responsible sources FSC® C102842

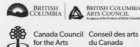

Greystone Books gratefully acknowledges the xʷməθkʷəy̓əm (Musqueam), Sḵwx̱wú7mesh (Squamish), and səlilwətaɬ (Tsleil-Waututh) peoples on whose land our Vancouver head office is located.

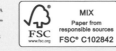

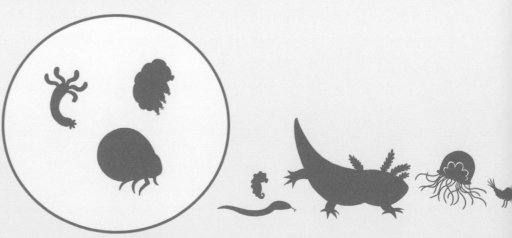

SUPER SMALL

Miniature Marvels of the Natural World

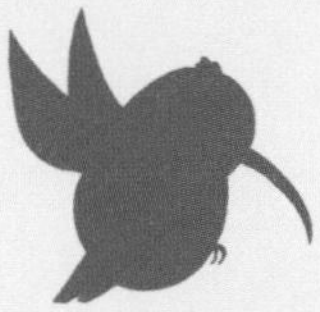

by
TIFFANY STONE

Illustrated by
ASHLEY SPIRES

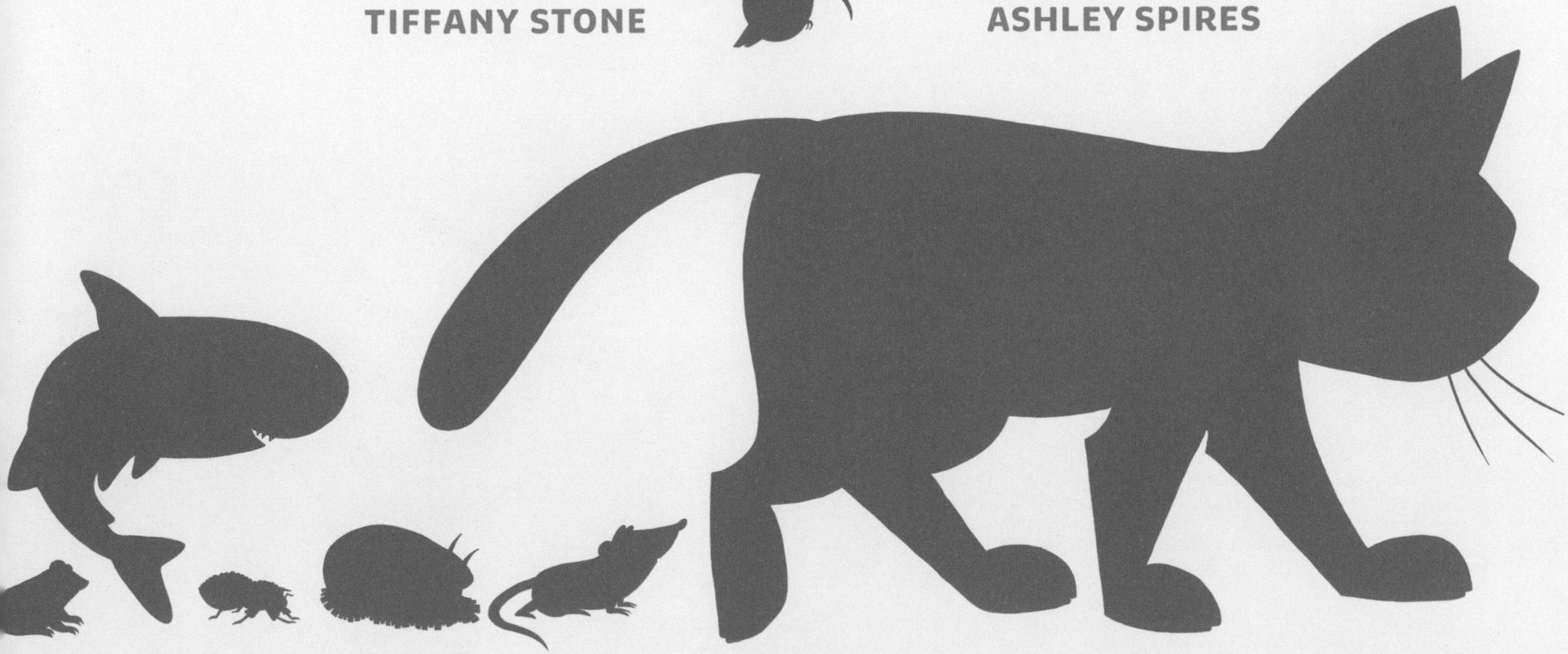

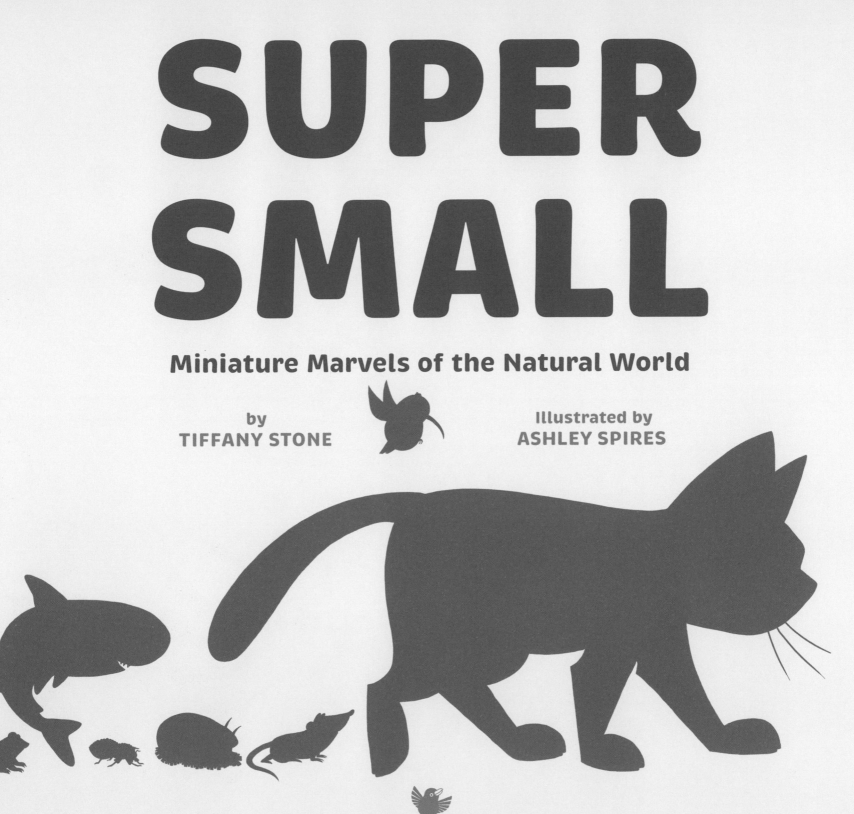

GREYSTONE KIDS
GREYSTONE BOOKS • VANCOUVER/BERKELEY/LONDON

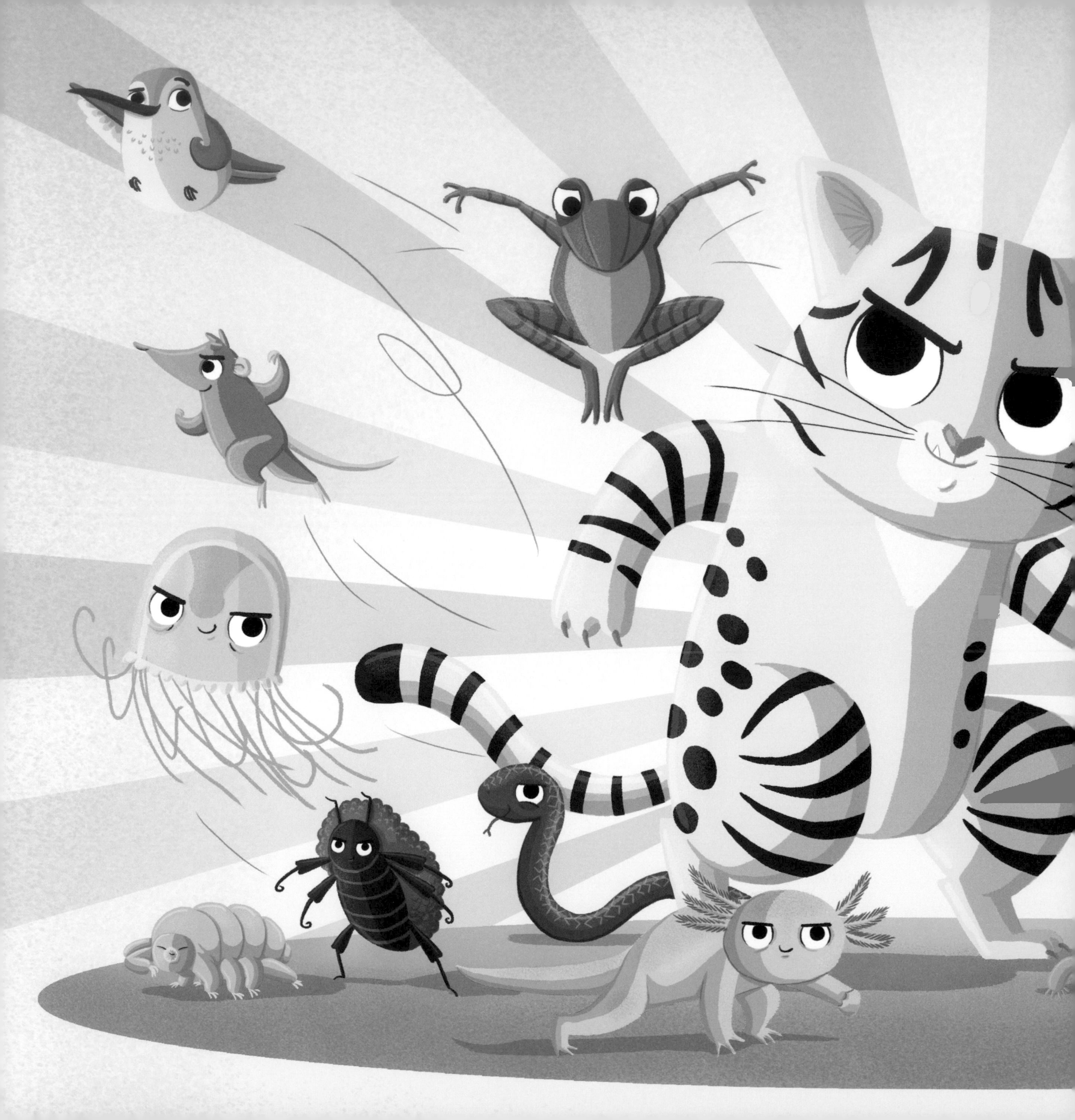

Superheroes, supervillains,
doin' deeds or simply chillin'.
Insects, reptiles, mammals, more,
with superpowers to explore.
And something else that's shared by all—
each, in its way, is . . .

super small.

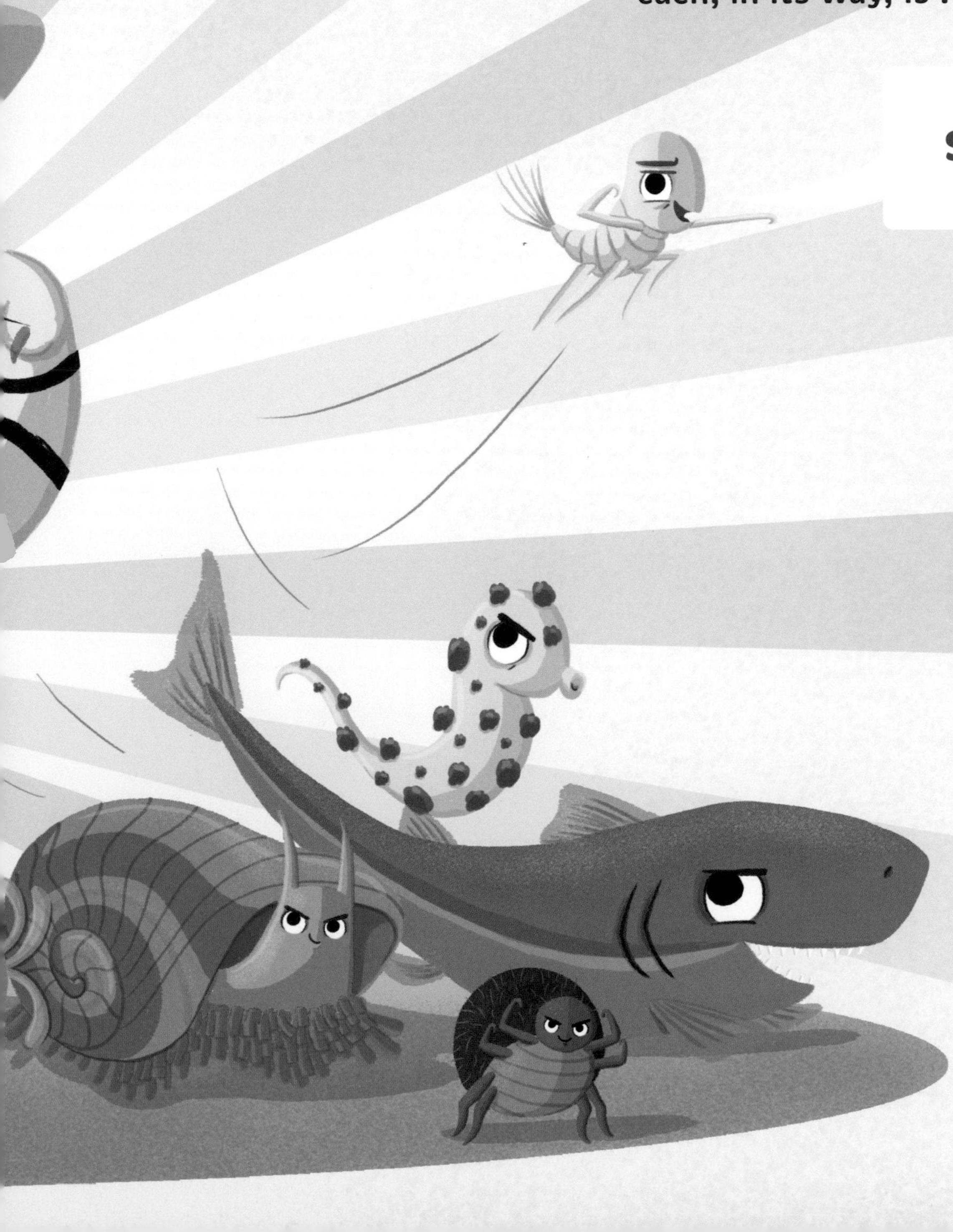

Oribatid Mite

Some mites might bite,
and some mites might not,
but this mite won't bite at all.

Not a bitey mite,
it's a mighty mite,
despite being mighty small.

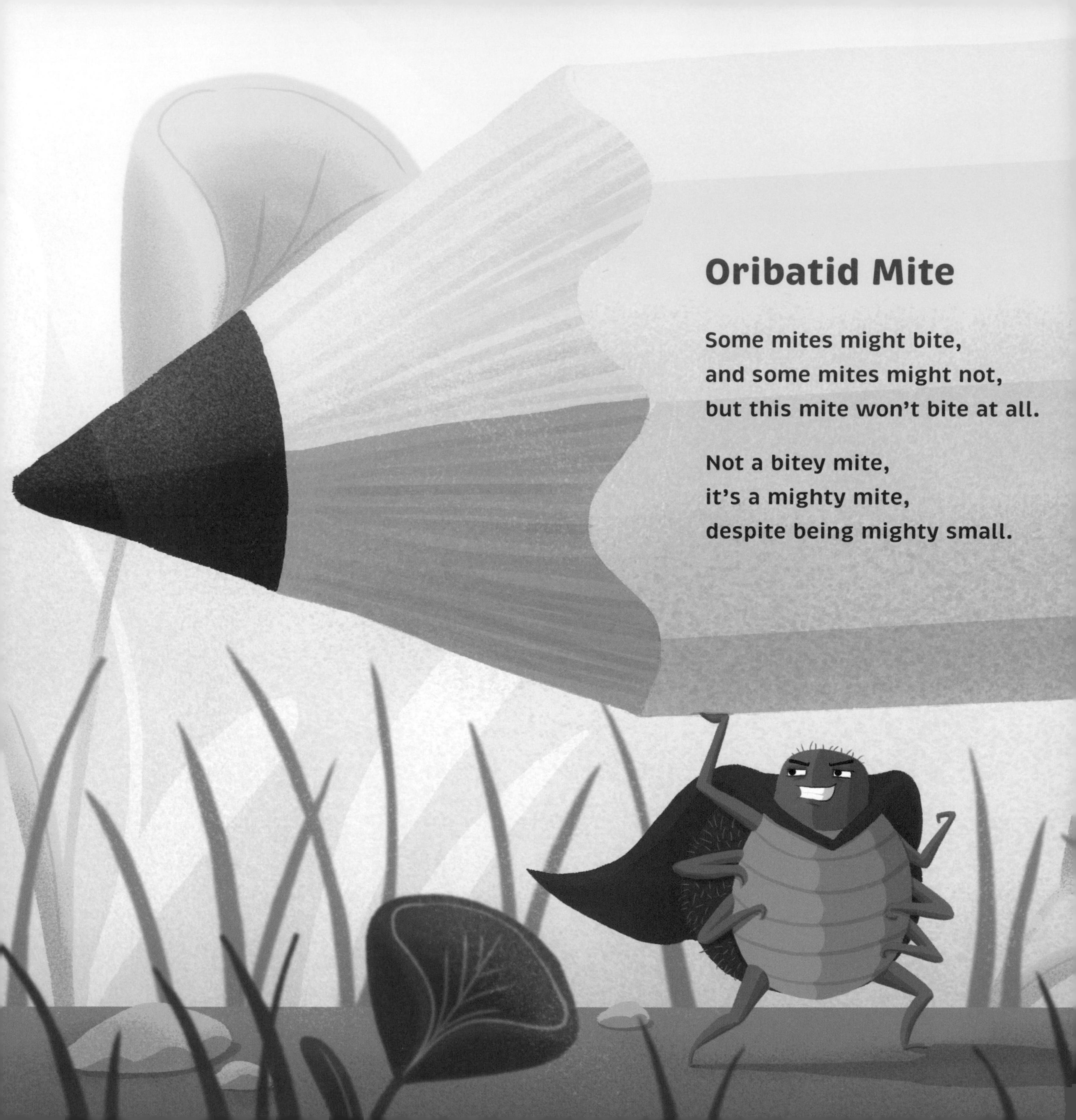

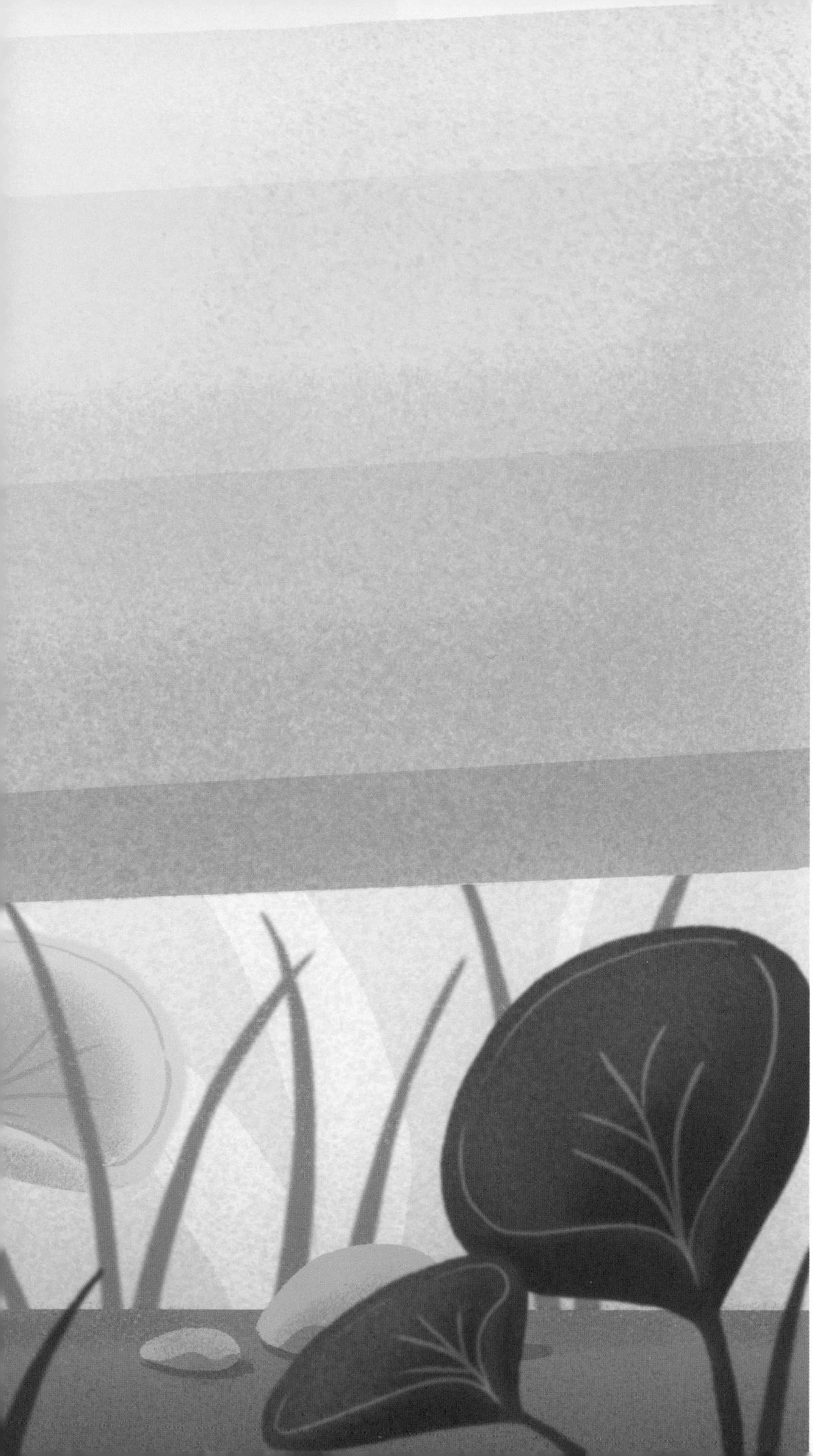

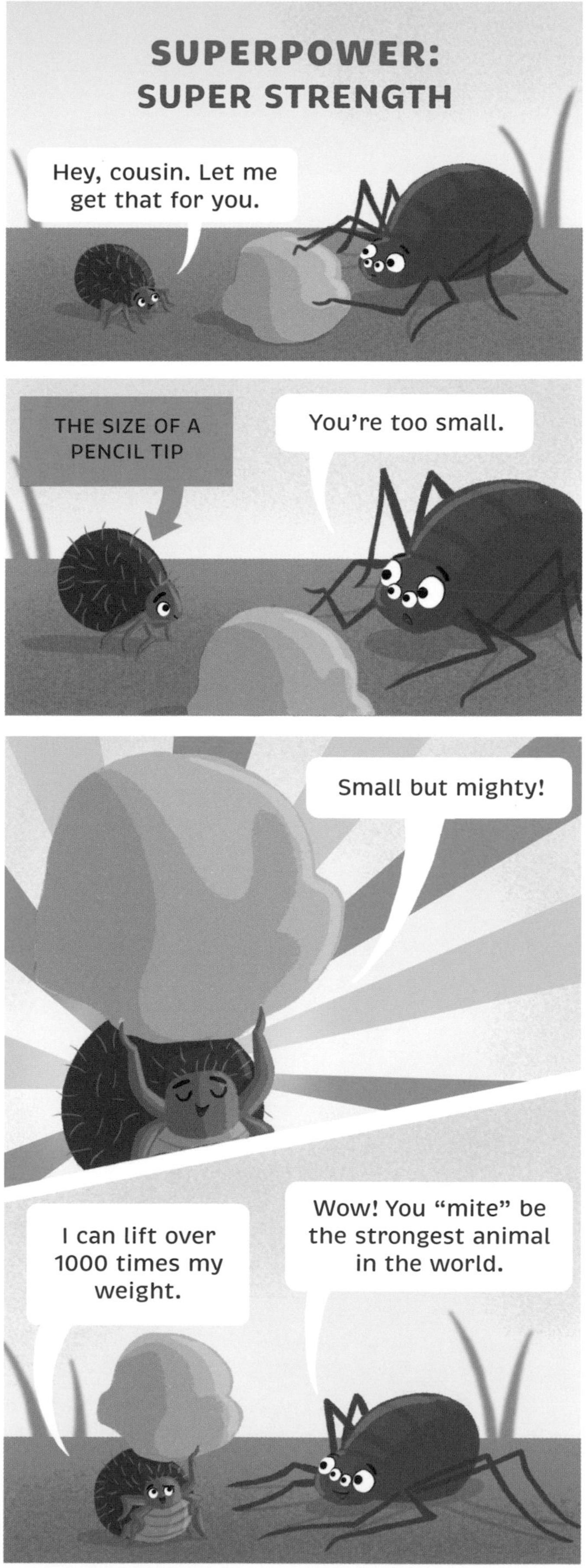
SUPERPOWER:
SUPER STRENGTH
Hey, cousin. Let me get that for you.
THE SIZE OF A PENCIL TIP
You're too small.
Small but mighty!
I can lift over 1000 times my weight.
Wow! You "mite" be the strongest animal in the world.

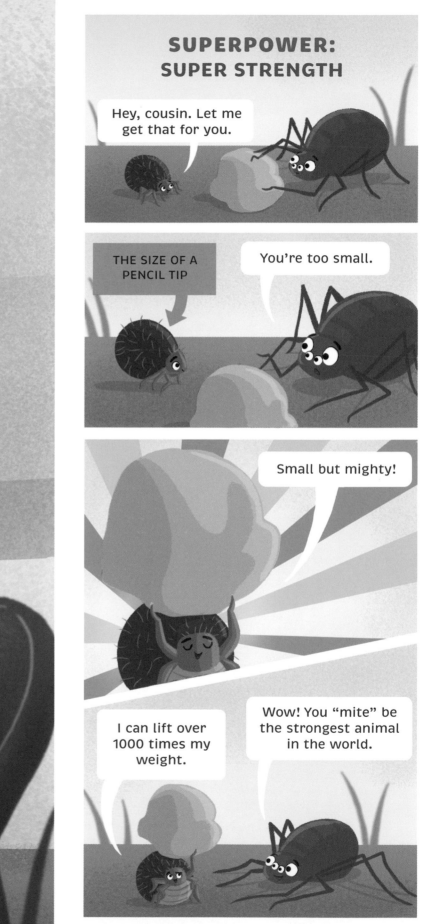

Pygmy Seahorse

Horses are little.
Horses are wee.
Dads give birth to babies
almost too small to see.

Horses are delicate.
Horses are frail.
A whole herd can hide
in my sandcastle pail.

Horses are miniature.
Horses are . . . what?!?
Oops, *sea*horses are little.
The *land* kind? They're not.

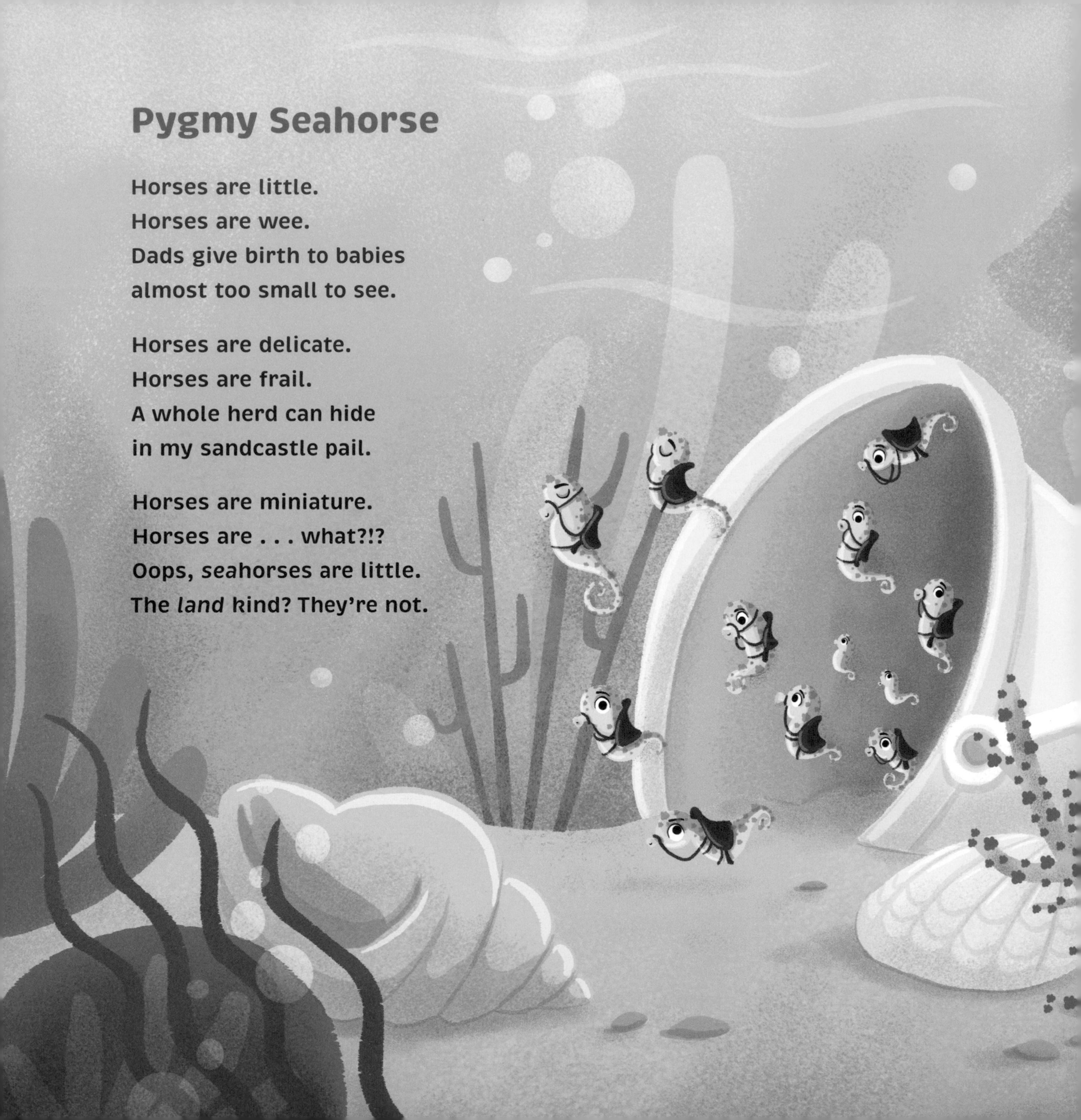

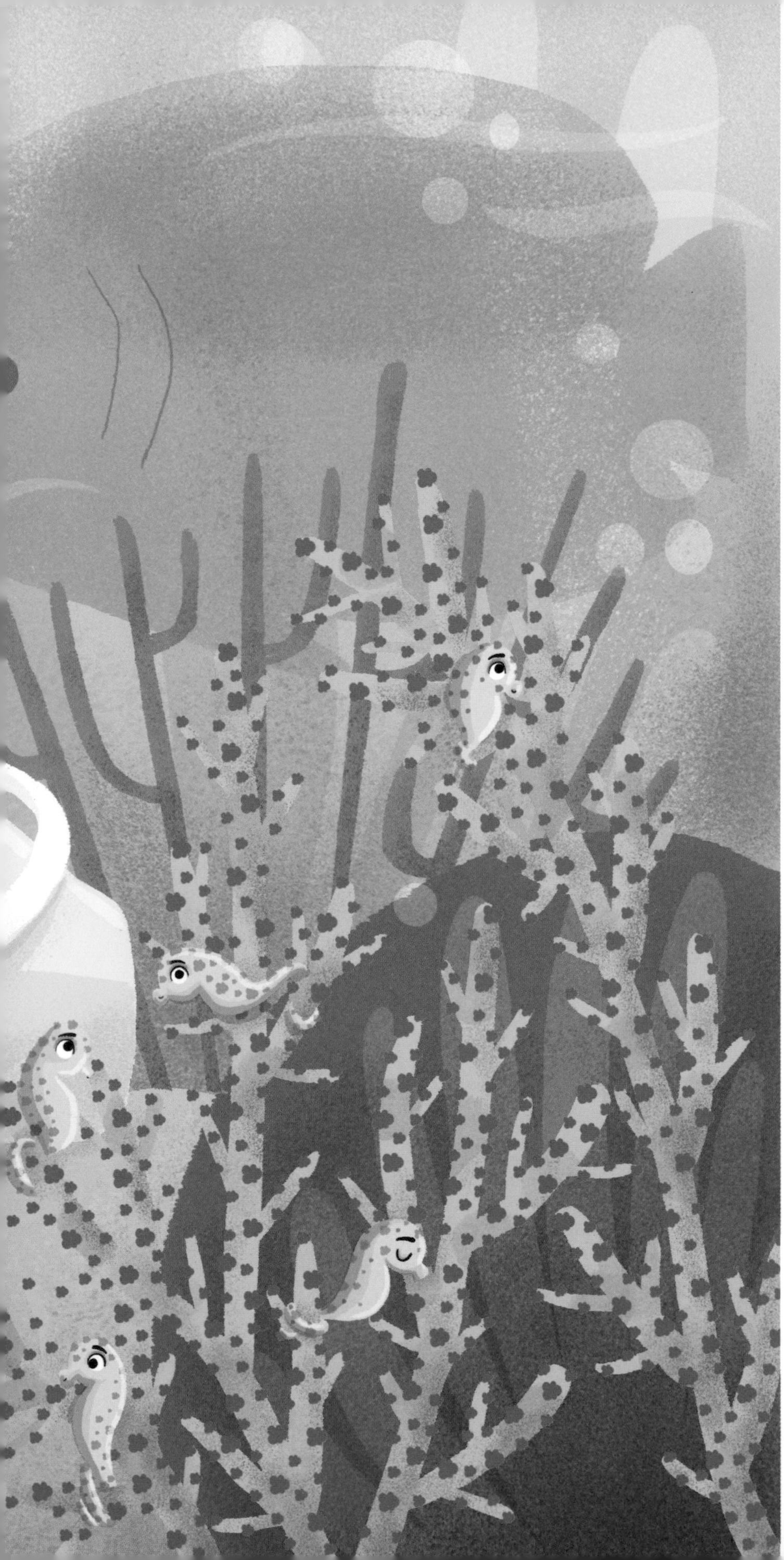

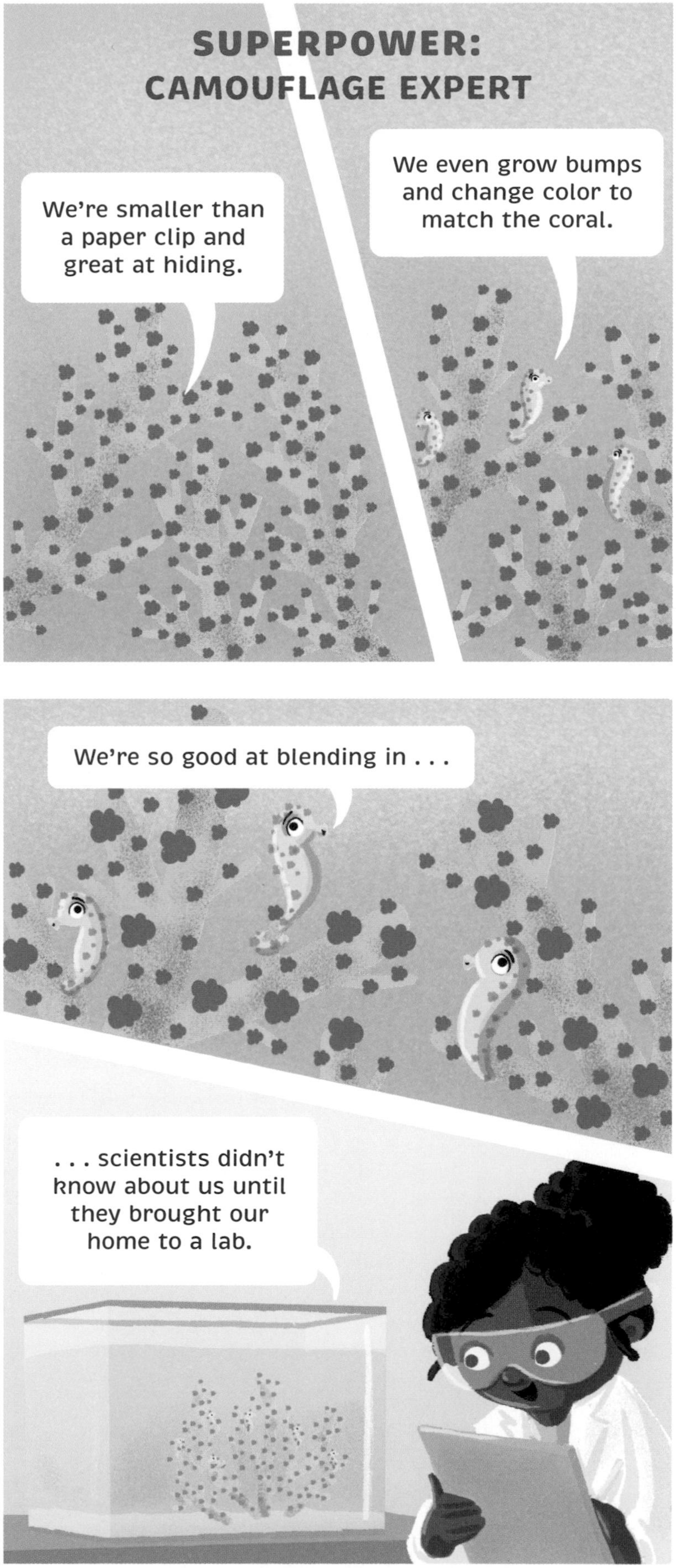
SUPERPOWER:
CAMOUFLAGE EXPERT
We're smaller than a paper clip and great at hiding.
We even grow bumps and change color to match the coral.
We're so good at blending in . . .
. . . scientists didn't know about us until they brought our home to a lab.

SUPERPOWER: GLOWS IN THE DARK

I'm the smallest shark . . .

SAME SIZE!

. . . and I glow in the dark.
That's called **bioluminescence**.

BIOLUMINESCENCE:
THE ABILITY OF LIVING THINGS
TO GIVE OFF LIGHT

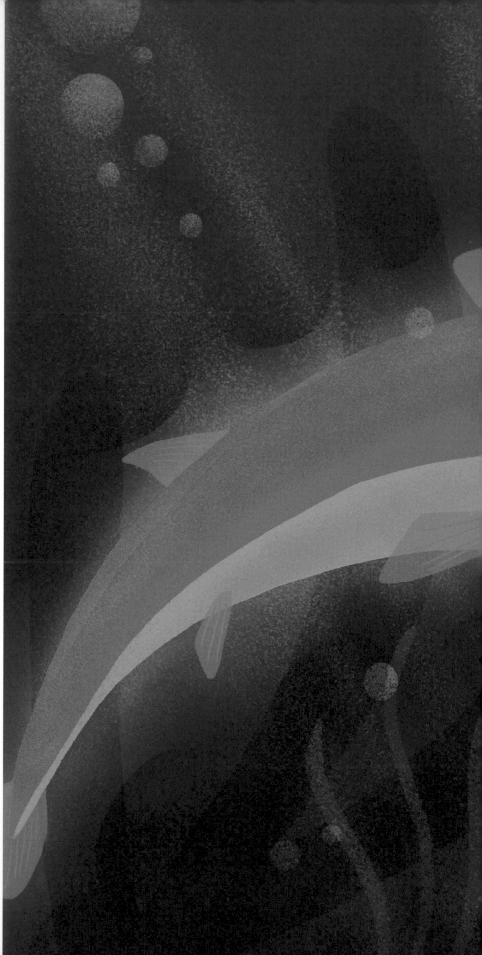

Dwarf Lantern Shark

In ocean depths,
in the twilight dark,
I lurk.

A dogfish, yes,
but I do not bark.
I hunt.

My body glows
like a neon spark.
I wait.

The smallest small,
still a hungry shark.
I . . .

CHOMP!

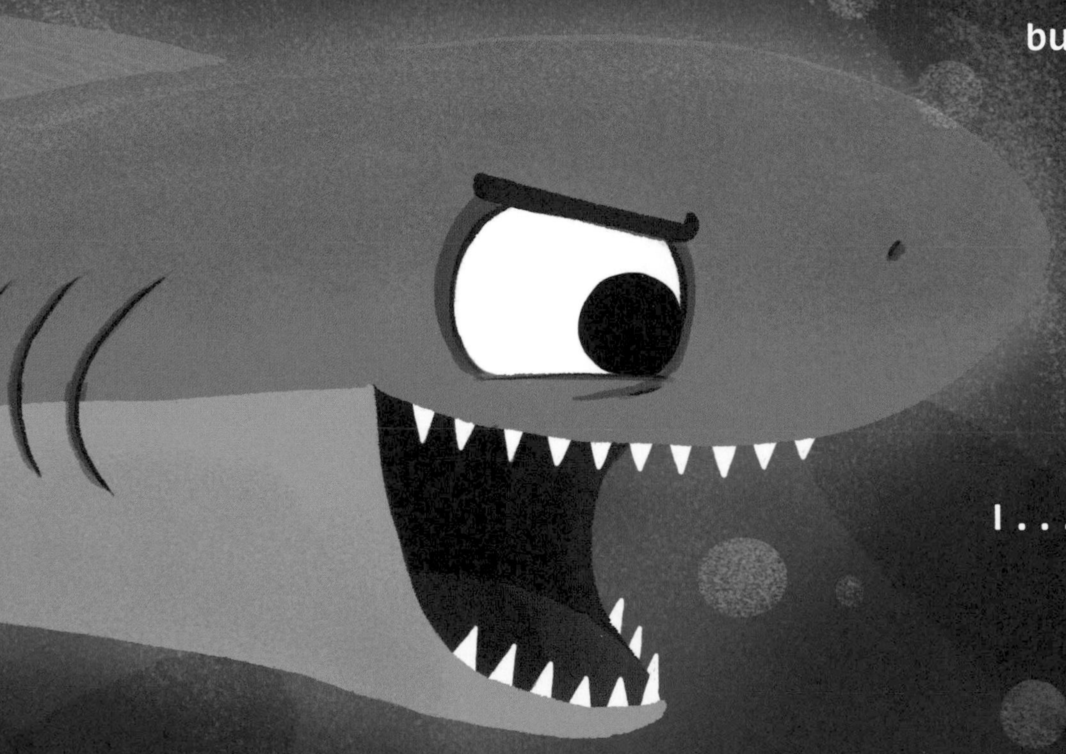

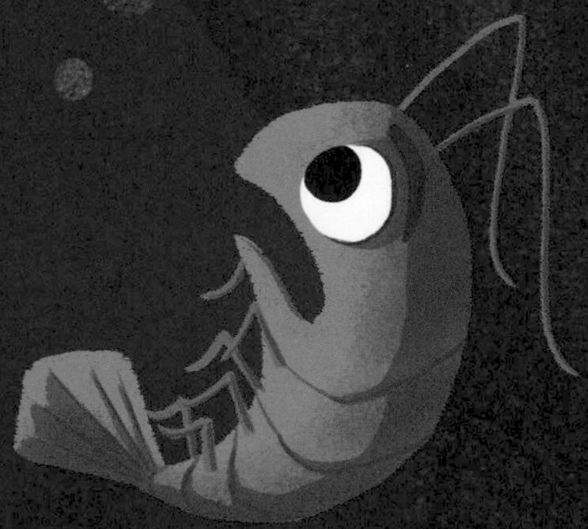

Axolotl

Why not ask an axolotl?
(Use your manners. Be polite.)
If you ask an axolotl,
then that axolotl might
relax a lot and lend a hand
(or two or three or four)
for that helpful axolotl
can easily grow more.

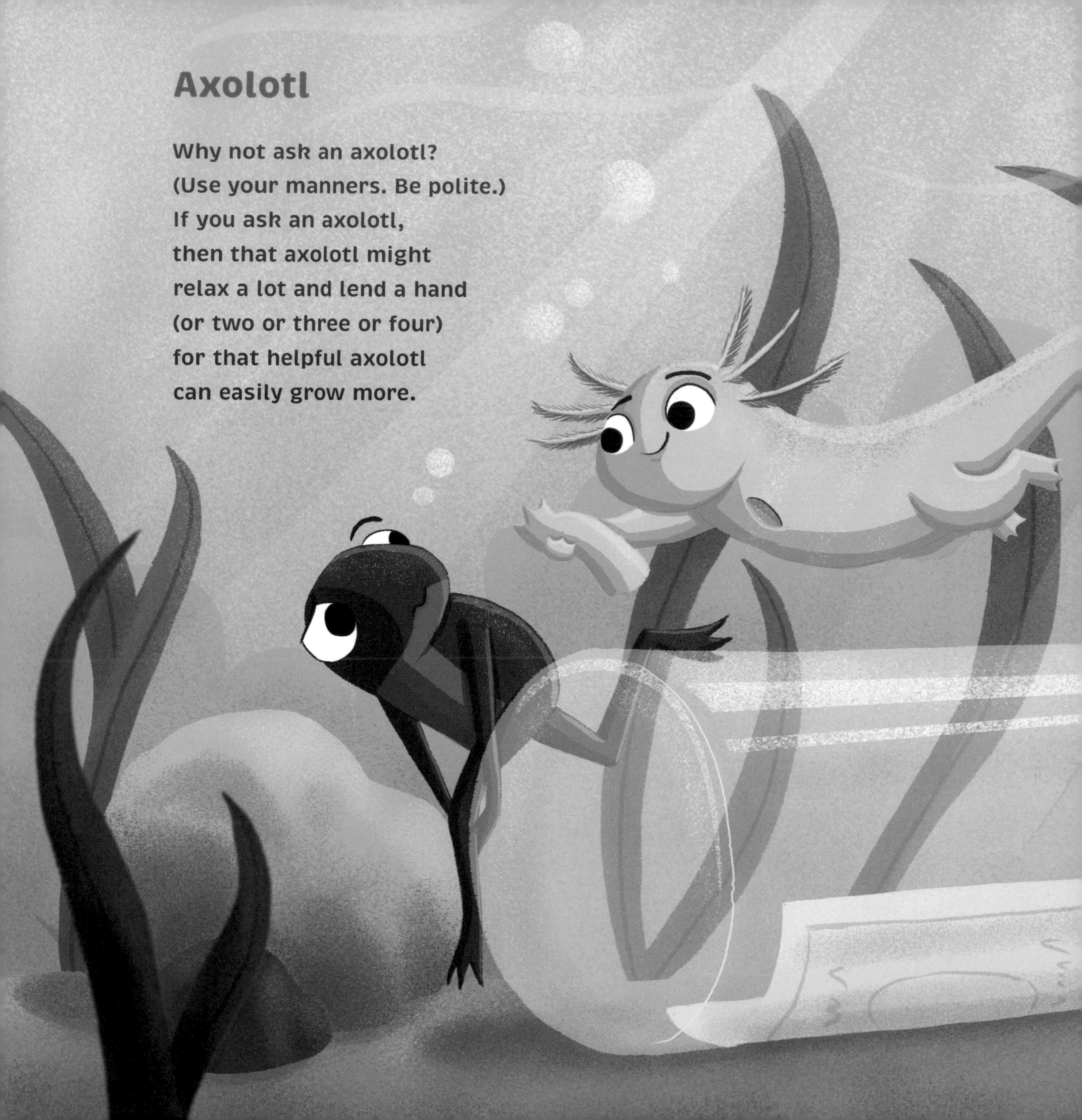

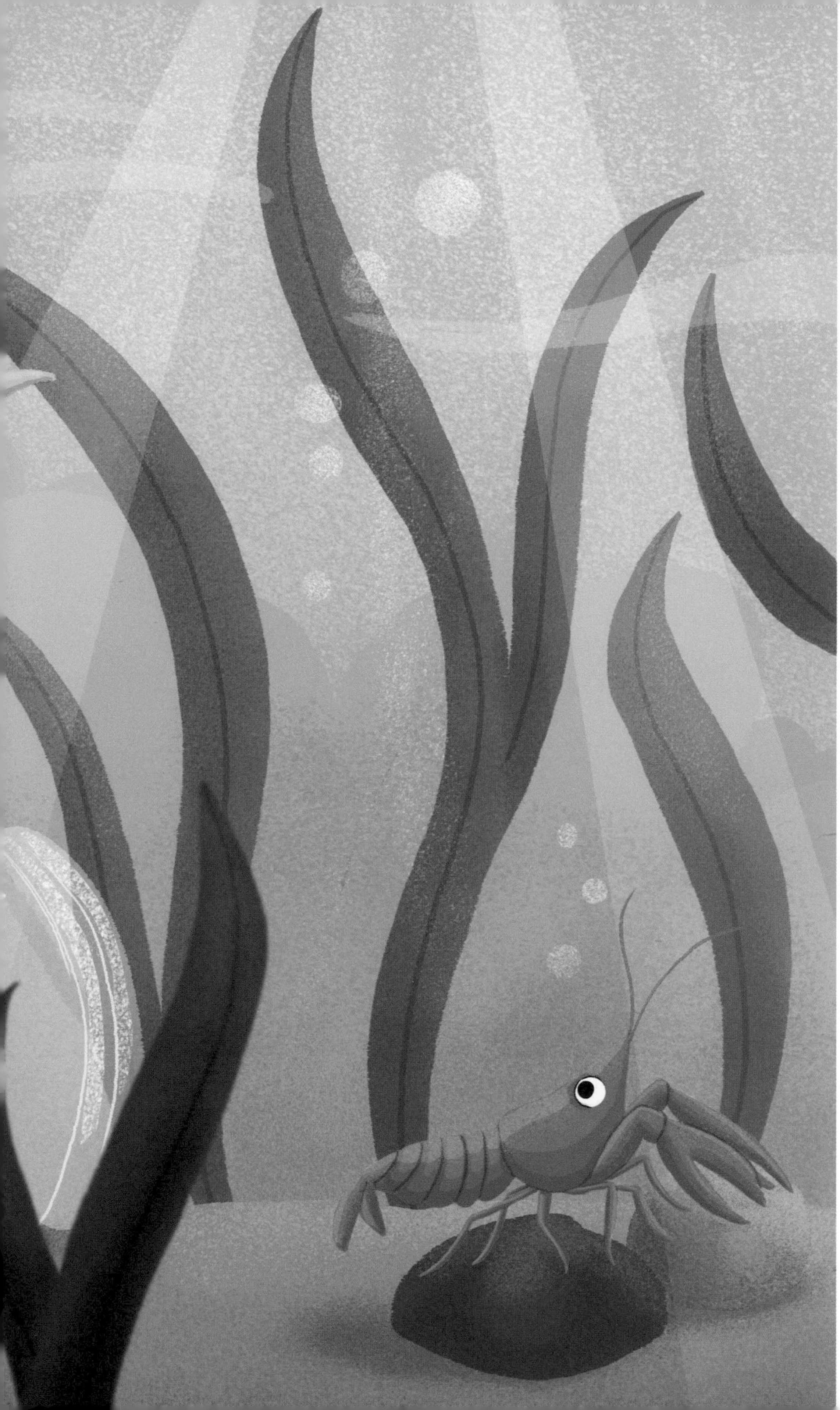

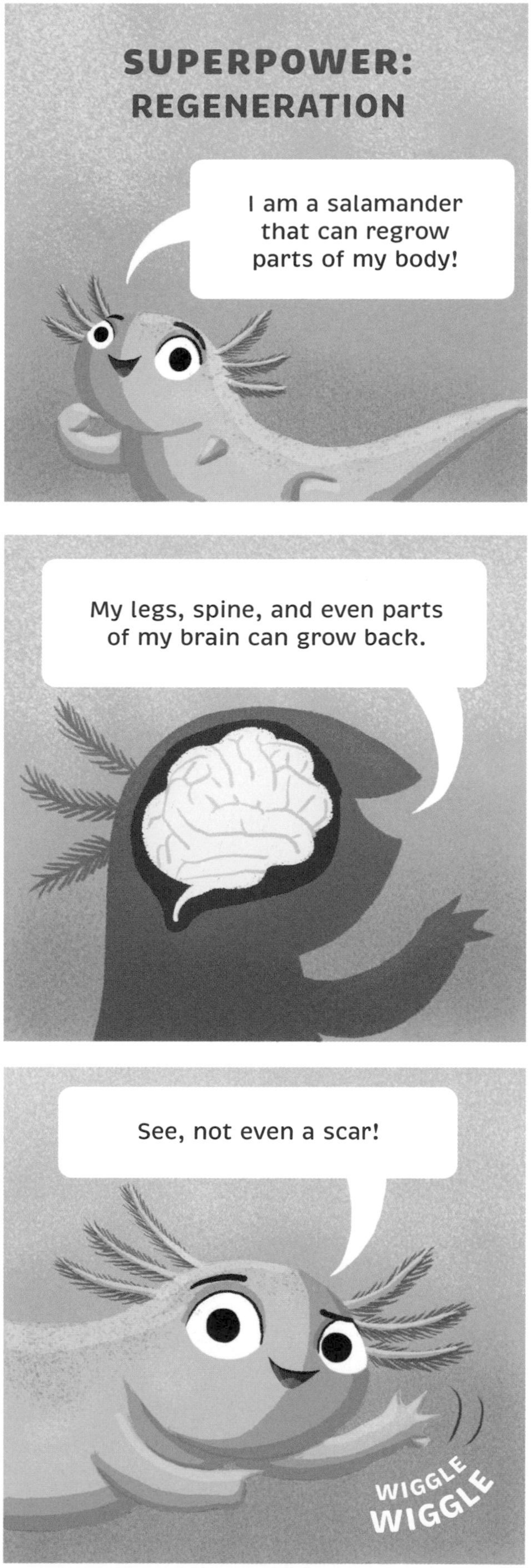
SUPERPOWER: REGENERATION
I am a salamander that can regrow parts of my body!
My legs, spine, and even parts of my brain can grow back.
See, not even a scar!
WIGGLE WIGGLE

Black-Footed Cat

An itty-bitty wild cat kitty,
sporting spots and stripes. So pretty!
Tiny toes on black-soled paws
and teensy teeth . . . in lethal jaws!

An itty-bitty wild cat kitty—
fearsome feline has no pity.
Best at hunting, deadly brute,
this itty kitty's killer cute!

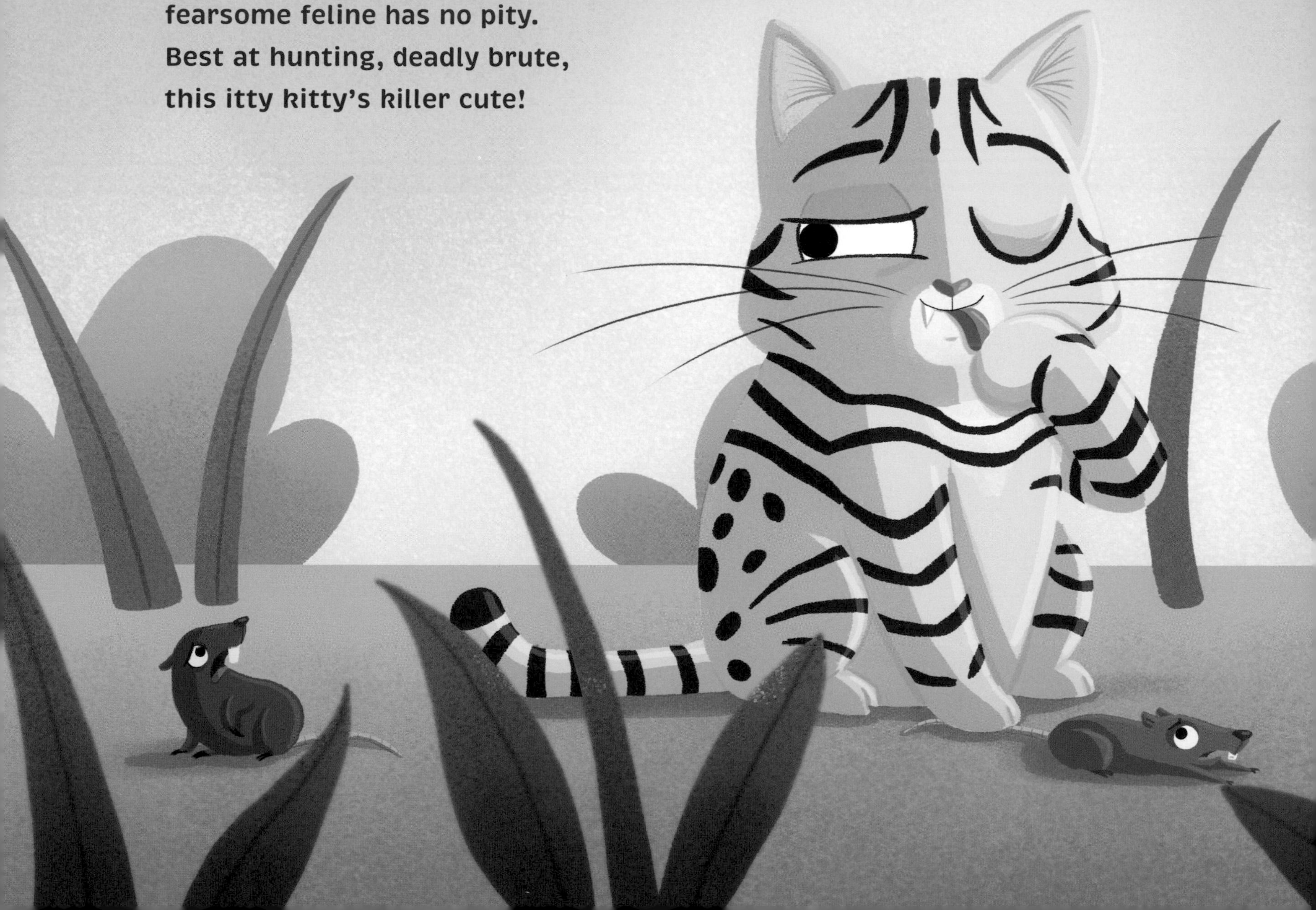

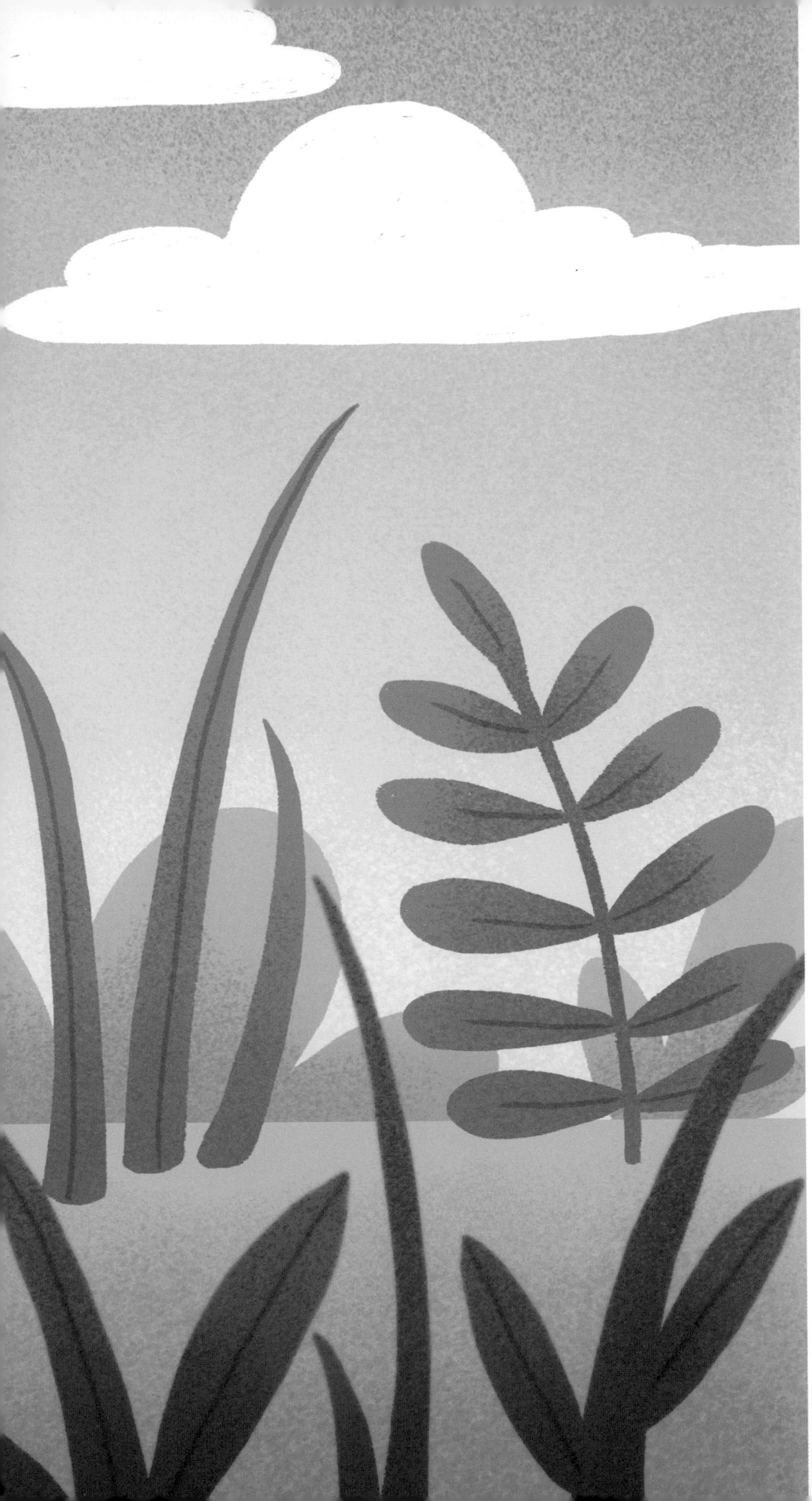

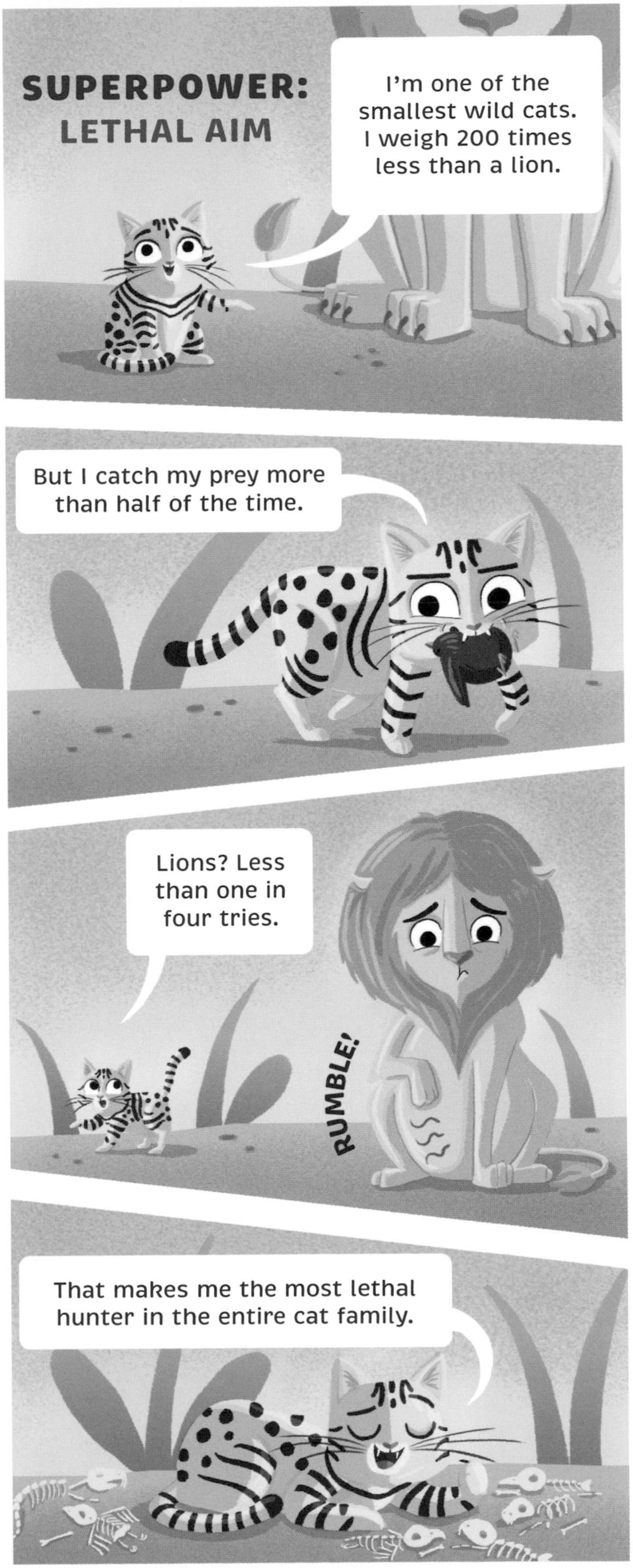
SUPERPOWER:
LETHAL AIM
I'm one of the smallest wild cats. I weigh 200 times less than a lion.
But I catch my prey more than half of the time.
Lions? Less than one in four tries.
RUMBLE!
That makes me the most lethal hunter in the entire cat family.

Scaly-Foot Snail

Clinkity-clank. Clinkity-clank.
I glide deep down in the sea.
Dressed in armor from shell to foot,
from foot to shell, that's me.

Clinkity-clank. Clinkity-clank.
The snail all snails want to be.
An iron-plated escargot.
See how my enemies flee!

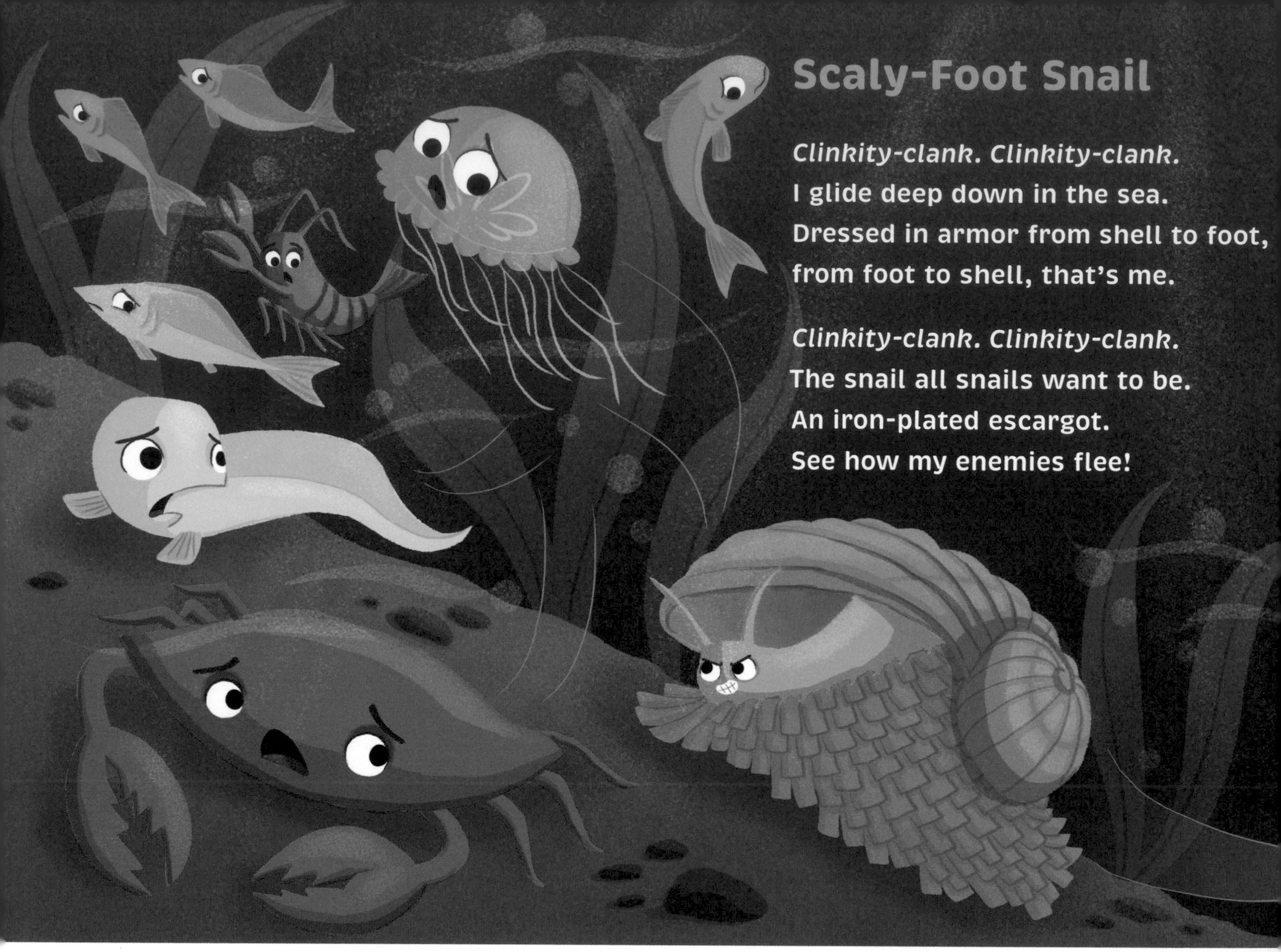

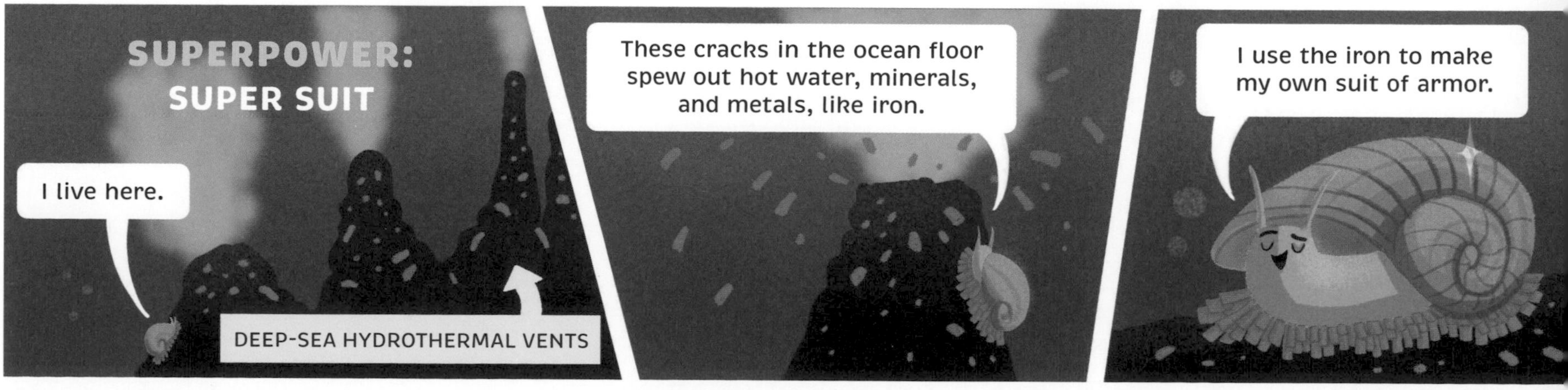

SUPERPOWER:
SUPER SUIT
I live here.
DEEP-SEA HYDROTHERMAL VENTS
These cracks in the ocean floor spew out hot water, minerals, and metals, like iron.
I use the iron to make my own suit of armor.

Plant Hopper

Look here!
I've got gears on my tiny rear hoppers.
When these rear gears sproing . . .
. . . ratchet . . .
. . . ratchet . . .
. . . ratchet . . .
BOING!!!
. . . wee jumps turn into whoppers.

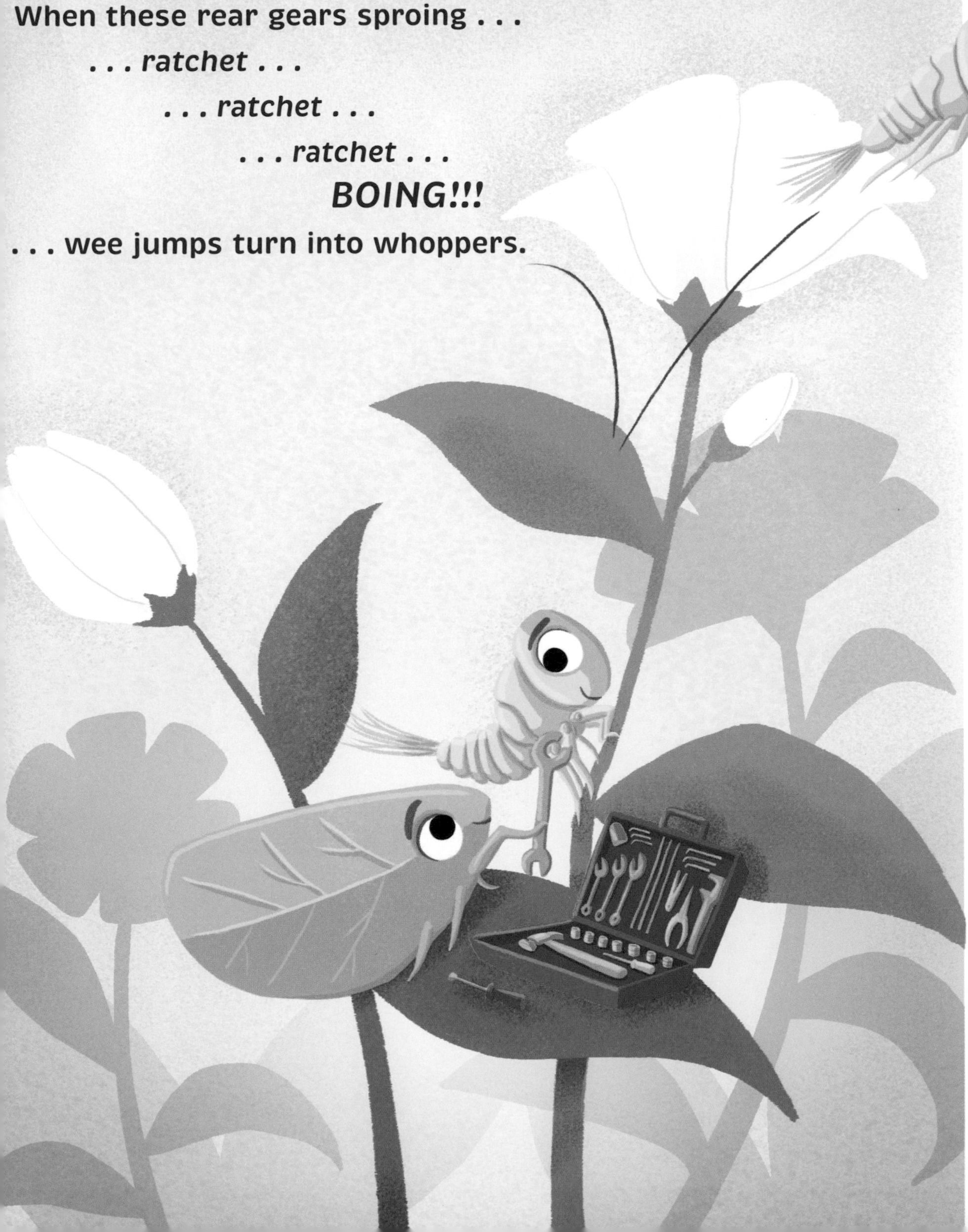

SUPERPOWER: REAR GEARS

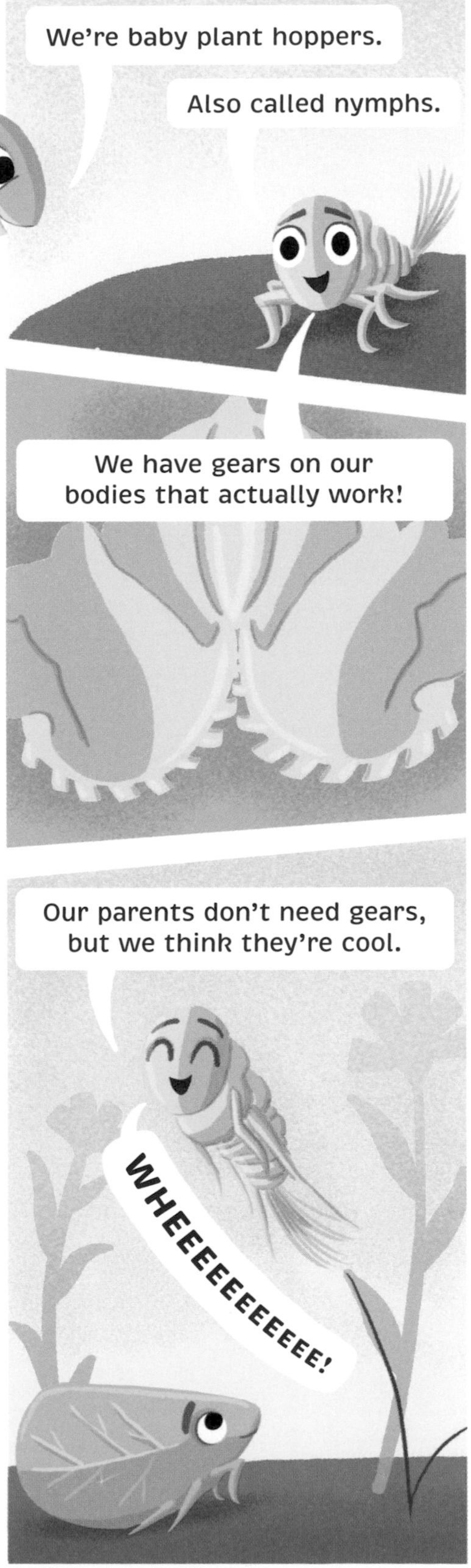
We're baby plant hoppers.
Also called nymphs.
We have gears on our bodies that actually work!
Our parents don't need gears, but we think they're cool.
WHEEEEEEEEEEE!

Bee Hummingbird

Nectar detector,
nectar inspector,
hover, hum, buzz.

Nectar selector,
nectar collector,
but not a bee because . . .

This backwards flier,
gravity defier
has feathers and not fuzz.

Turquoise attire,
wingbeats of fire,
bee hummingbird.

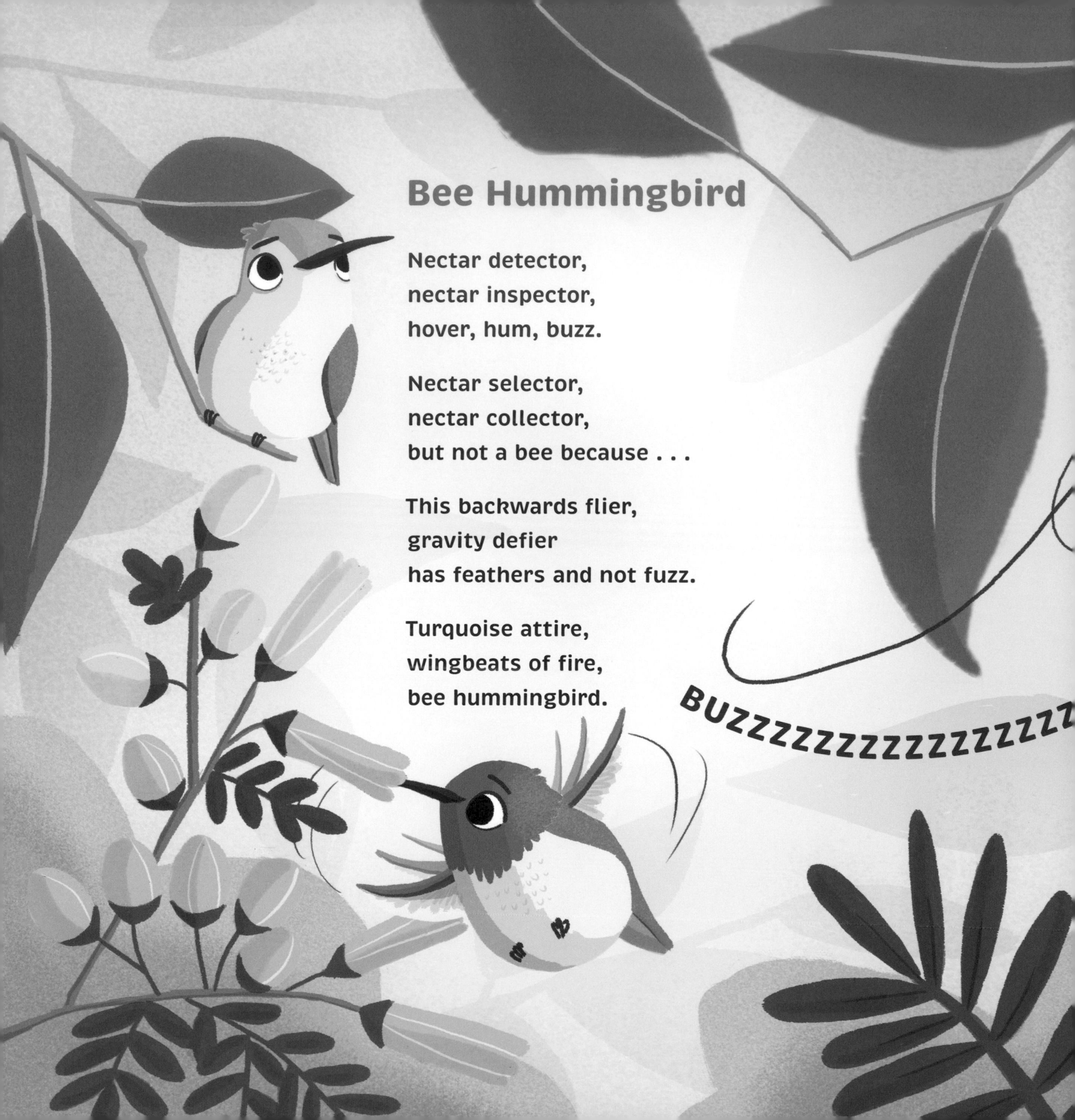
BUZZZZZZZZZZZZZZZZ

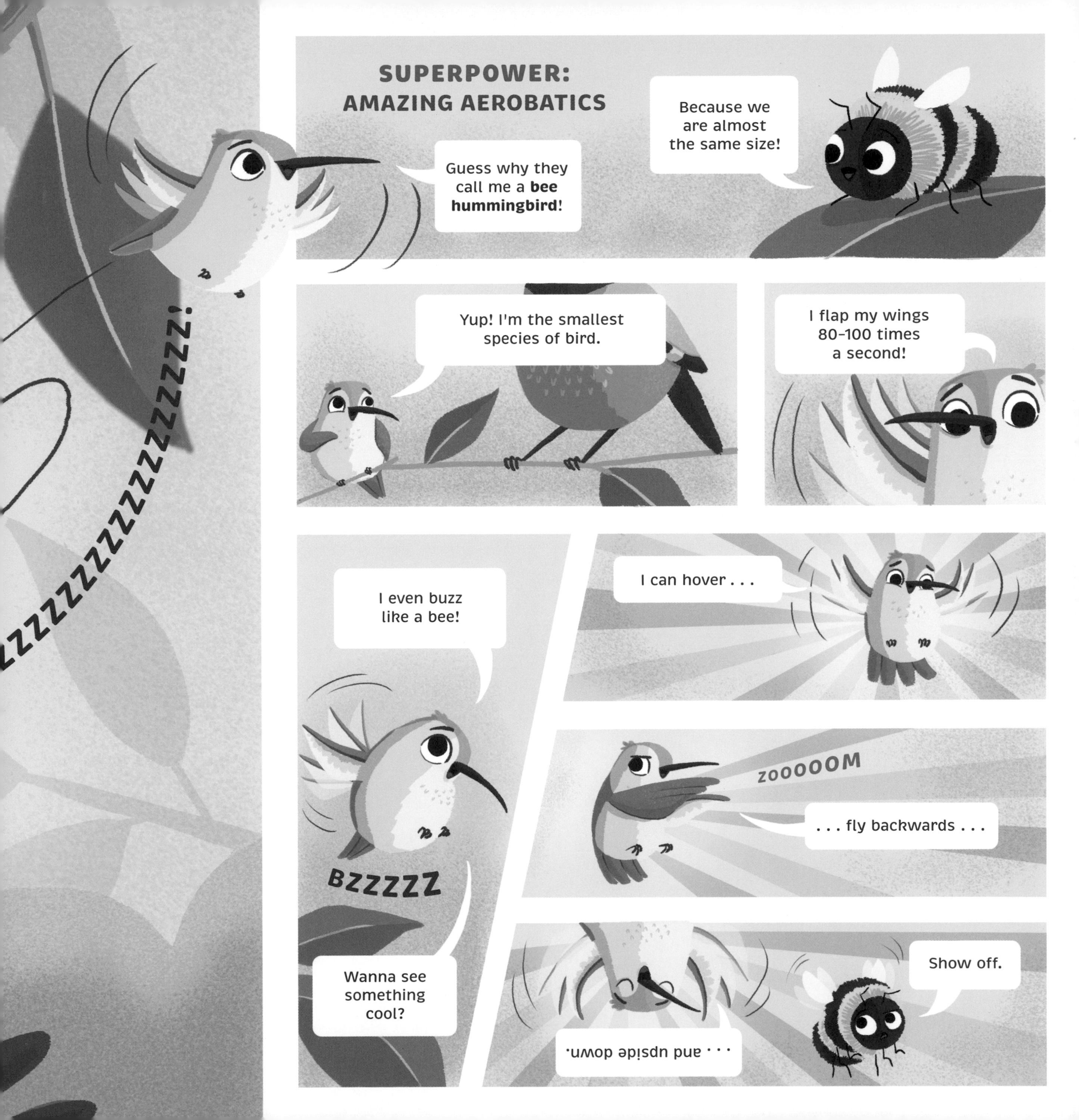

SUPERPOWER: AMAZING AEROBATICS
Guess why they call me a **bee hummingbird**!
Because we are almost the same size!
Yup! I'm the smallest species of bird.
I flap my wings 80–100 times a second!
I even buzz like a bee!
BZZZZZ
Wanna see something cool?
I can hover . . .
ZOOOOOM
. . . fly backwards . . .
. . . and upside down.
Show off.

Hydra

Hi there, I'm a hydra. I look FABULOUS, I know.
Can you believe I don't need help to get this youthful glow?
No lotions, creams, or powders. No filters on my phone.
Every day I look this great *completely* on my own.
And even more astounding, I'll never age a day,
because I am a hydra, and we're simply born that way.

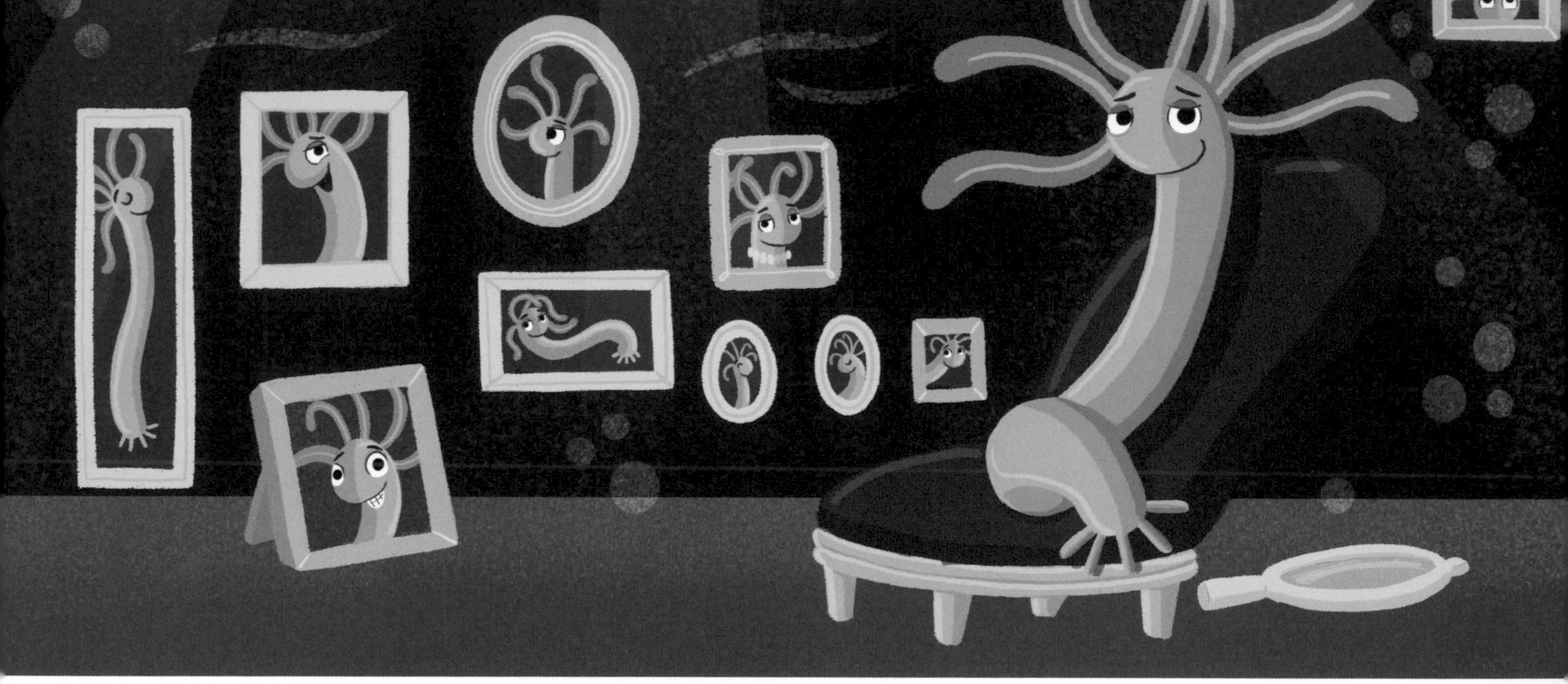

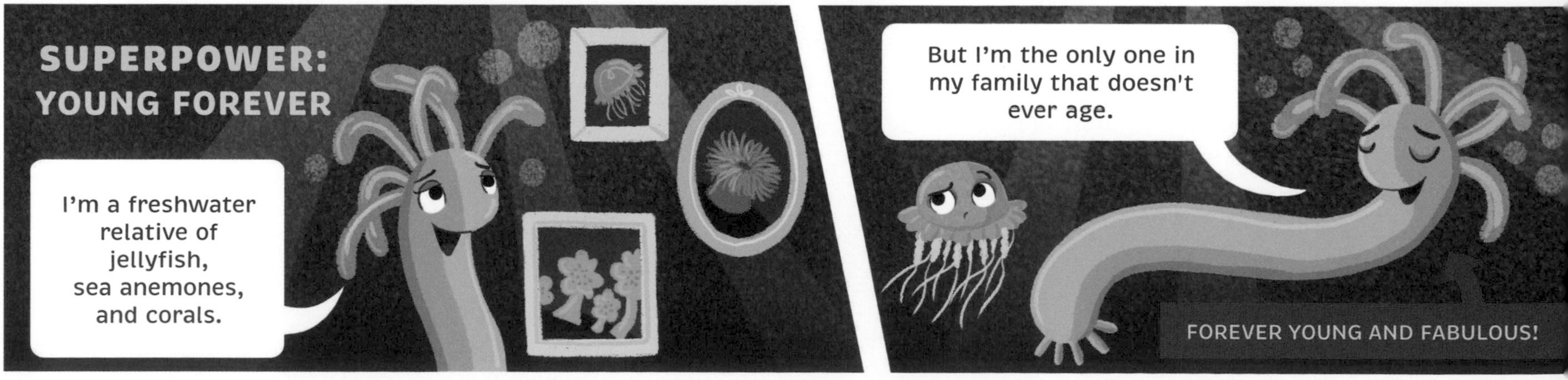
SUPERPOWER: YOUNG FOREVER
I'm a freshwater relative of jellyfish, sea anemones, and corals.
But I'm the only one in my family that doesn't ever age.
FOREVER YOUNG AND FABULOUS!

Diabolical Ironclad Beetle

Diabolical Ironclad Beetle. Indestructible by cars and people. Supervillain or superhero? Diabolical Ironclad Beetle.

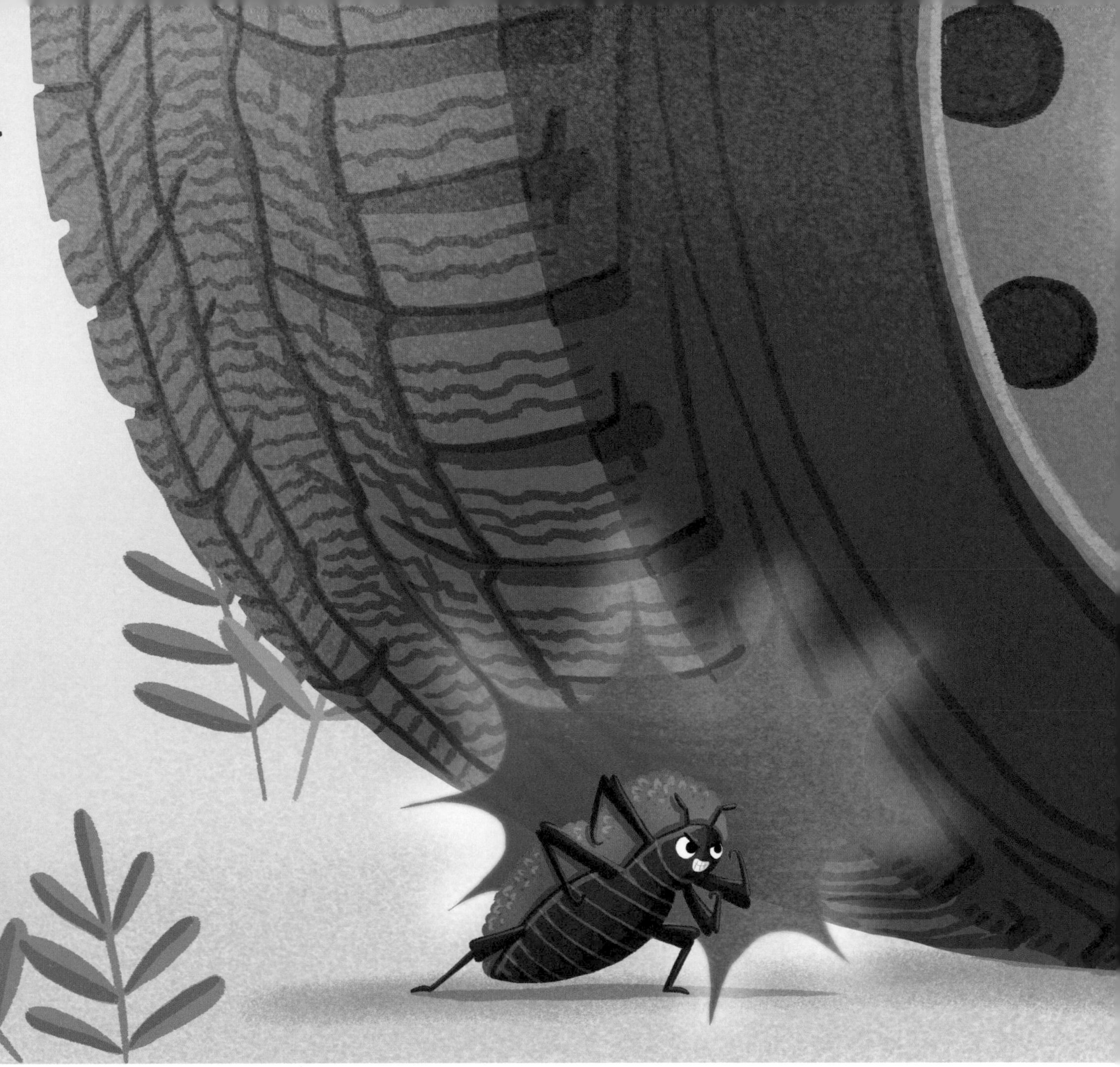

SUPERPOWER: CRUSH RESISTANT

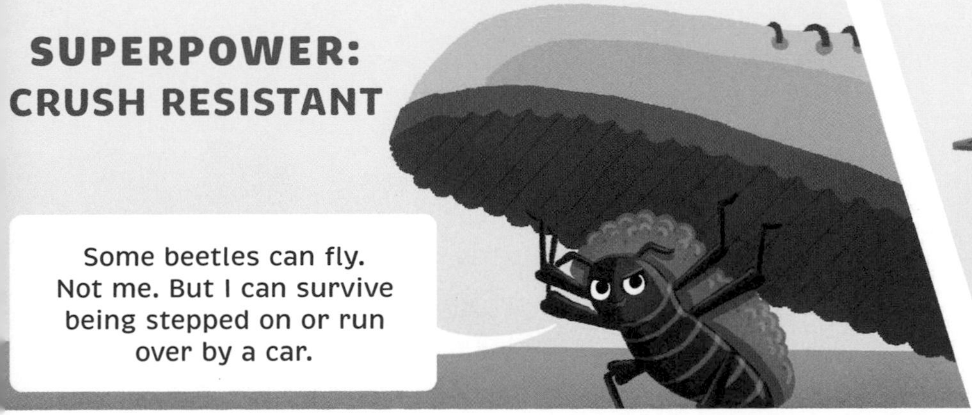

Some beetles can fly. Not me. But I can survive being stepped on or run over by a car.

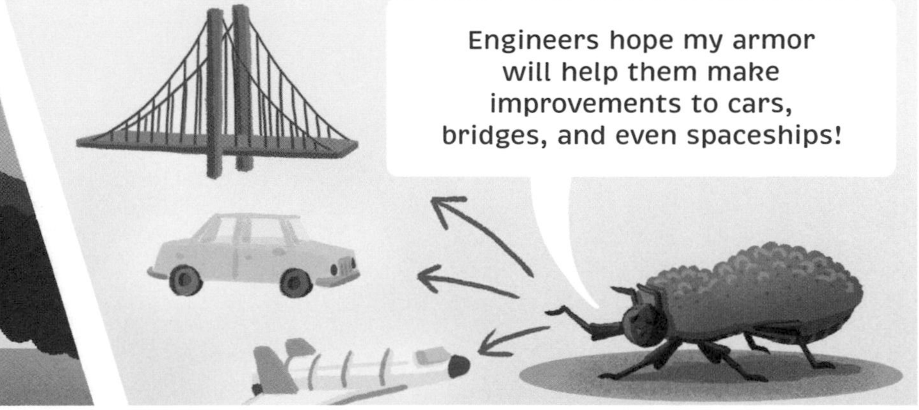

Engineers hope my armor will help them make improvements to cars, bridges, and even spaceships!

Immortal Jellyfish

Picture it now: a mom or a dad
who is having the worst day that they've ever had.
But instead of collapsing from stress or from pain—
POOF! What the heck?! They're a baby again.
And this restart repeats every time they face strife,
so they don't ever quit, they just reboot their life.

Now I know that you know this is not how it goes,
at least not for humans. No, never for those.
But one kind of jellyfish, tiny and clever,
does *really* renew—and might do so *forever* . . .

SUPERPOWER: INFINITE REBOOTS

Stressed? Injured? Old? No big deal.

I just concentrate and . . .

Voila!

POLYP (BABY JELLYFISH)

I simply go back to being a baby and grow up all over again.

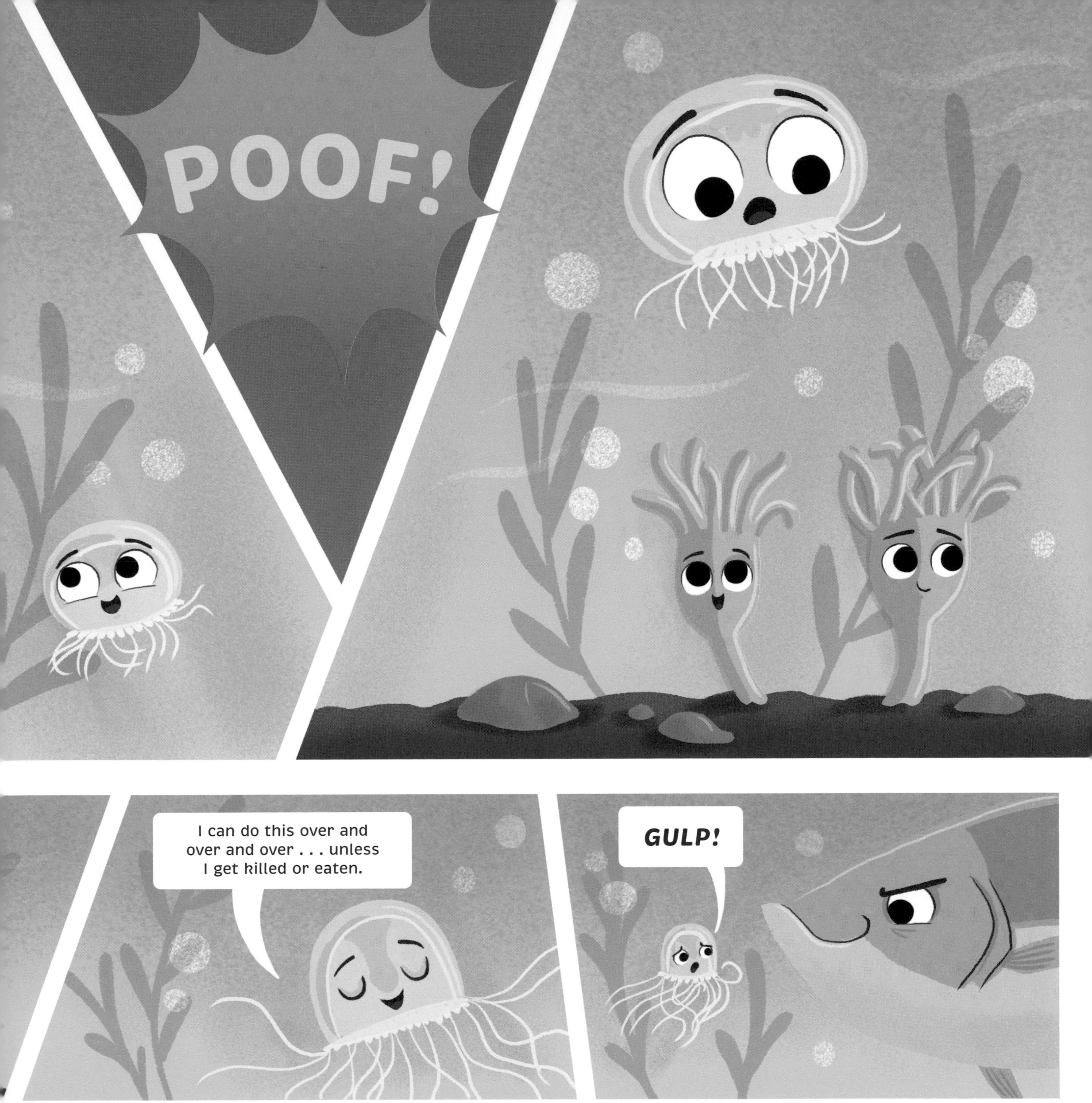
POOF!
I can do this over and over and over . . . unless I get killed or eaten.
GULP!

Etruscan Shrew

If you—yes, *you*—were an Etruscan shrew,
do you know, do you know, do you know what you'd do?
You would chew, chew, chew—chew the whole day through.
You would even eat up critters the same size as you!

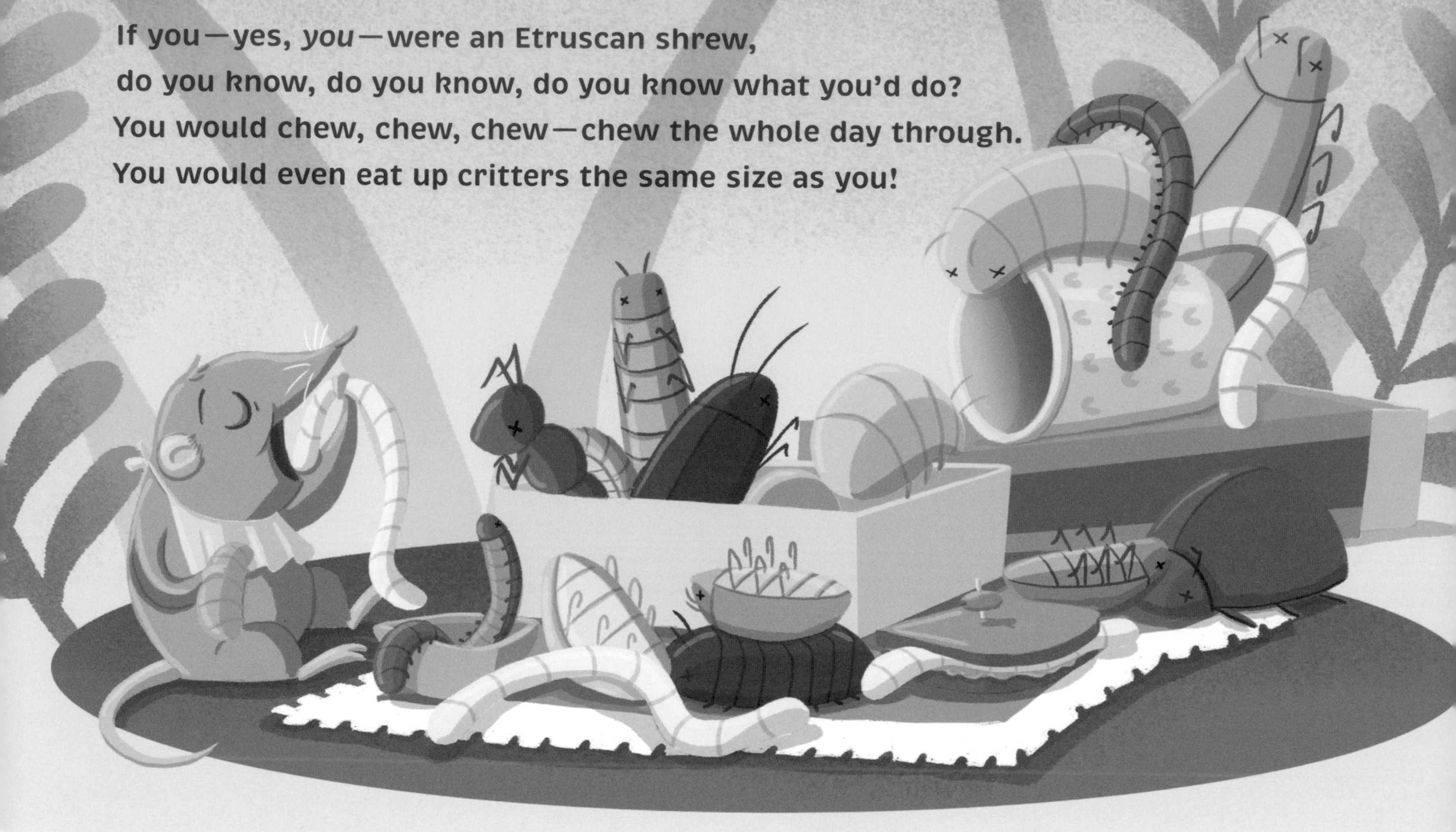

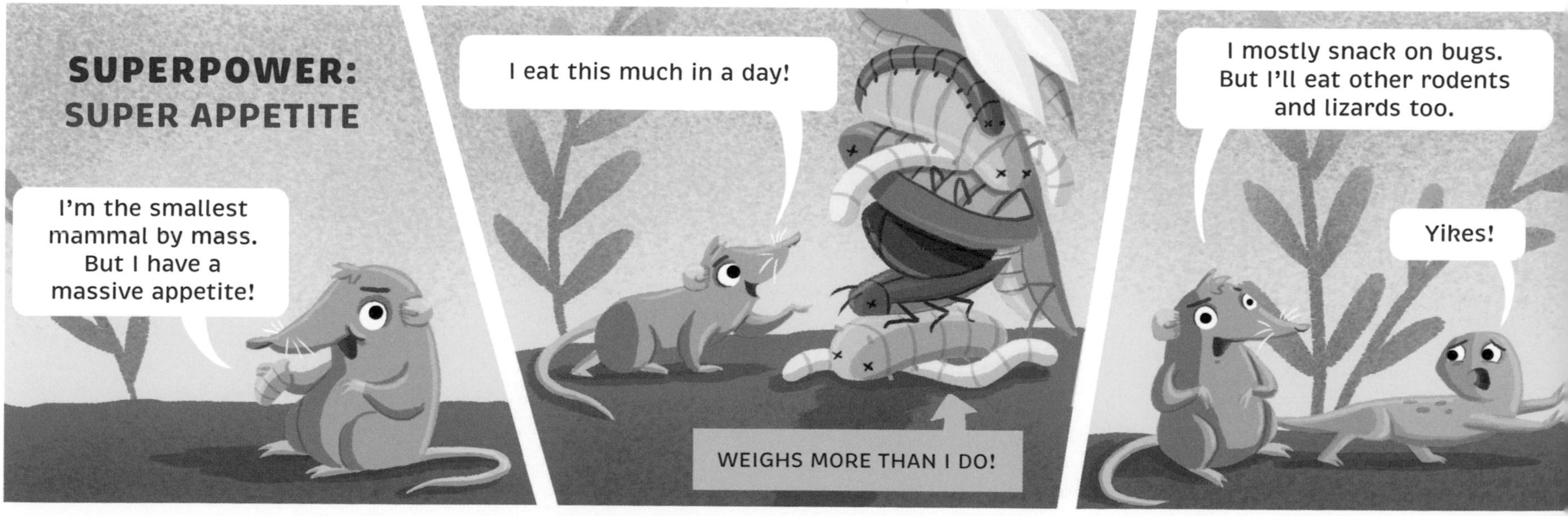

SUPERPOWER:
SUPER APPETITE
I'm the smallest mammal by mass. But I have a massive appetite!
I eat this much in a day!
WEIGHS MORE THAN I DO!
I mostly snack on bugs. But I'll eat other rodents and lizards too.
Yikes!

Wood Frog

Amphibian Popsicles?
Comical—
but actual,
not mythological.
When winter weather's untropical,
it's optimal,
biologically logical
for some frogs to be . . . Frogsicles!

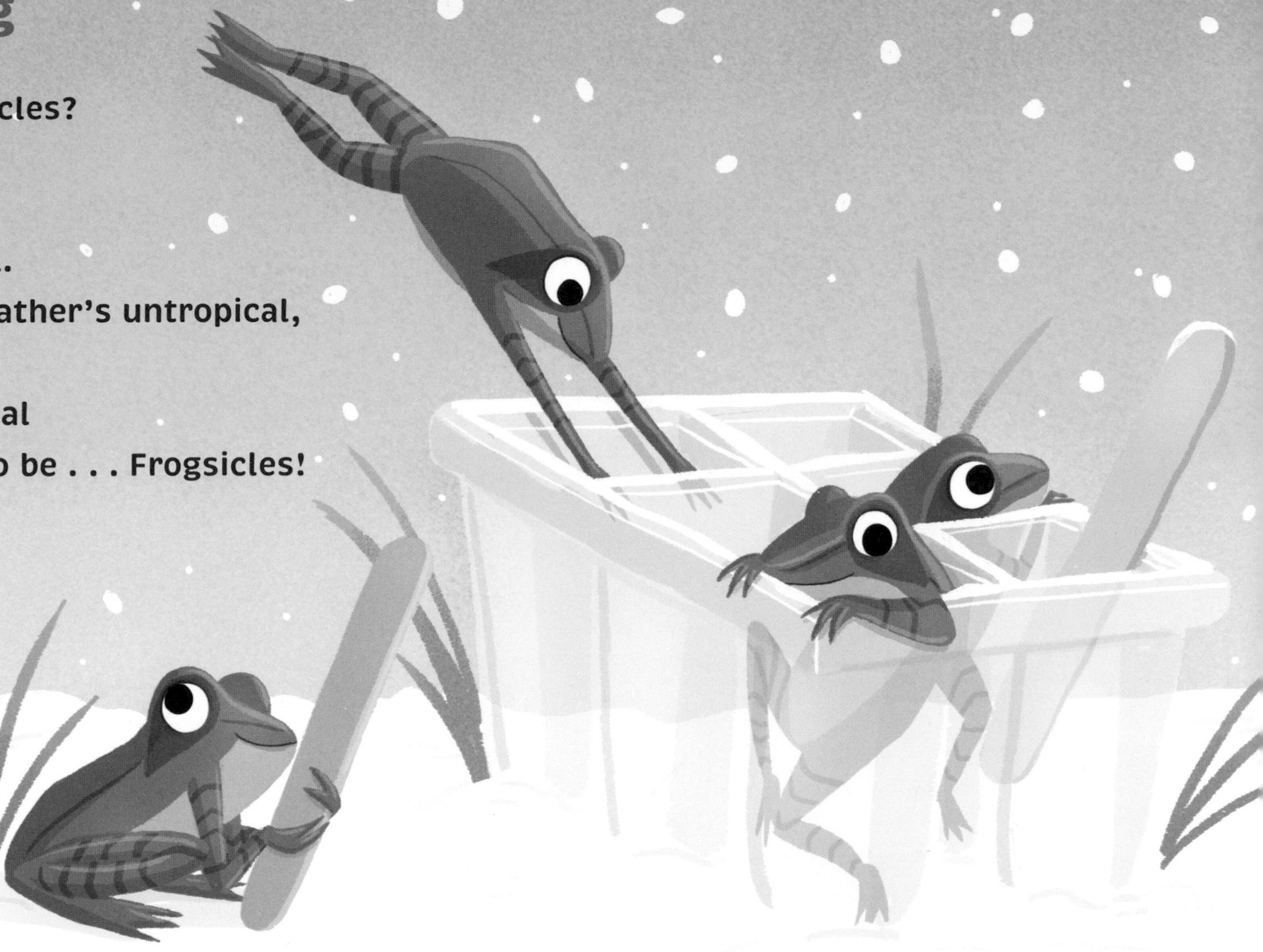

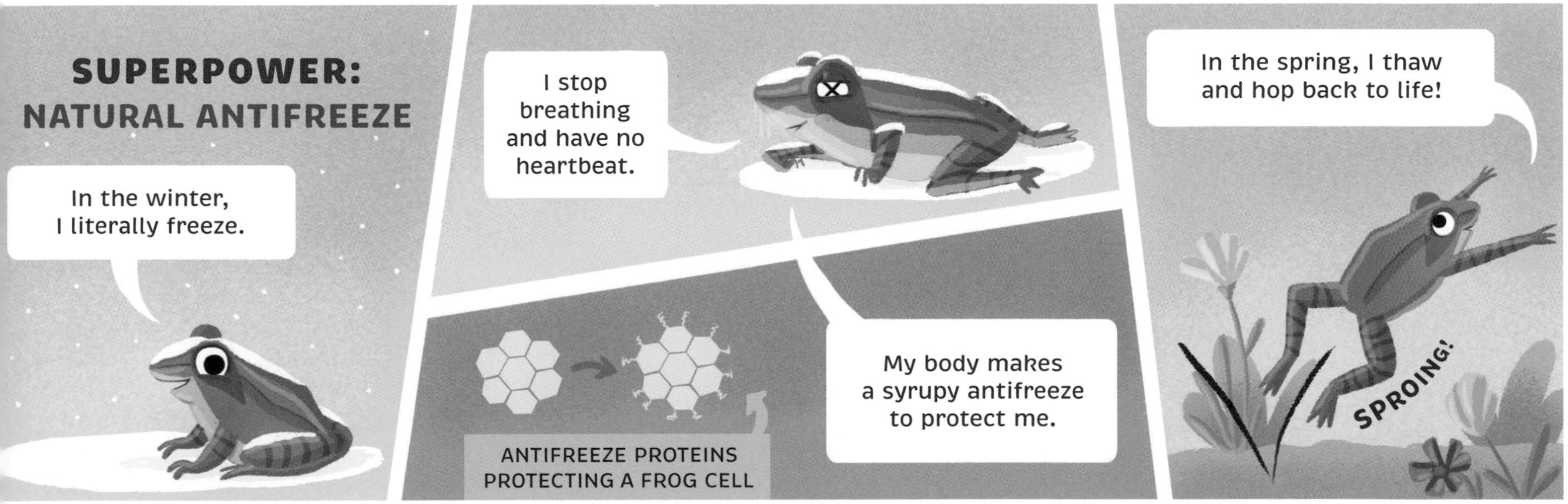

SUPERPOWER:
NATURAL ANTIFREEZE
In the winter, I literally freeze.
I stop breathing and have no heartbeat.
ANTIFREEZE PROTEINS PROTECTING A FROG CELL
My body makes a syrupy antifreeze to protect me.
In the spring, I thaw and hop back to life!
SPROING!

SUPERPOWER: SUPER SURVIVAL SKILLS

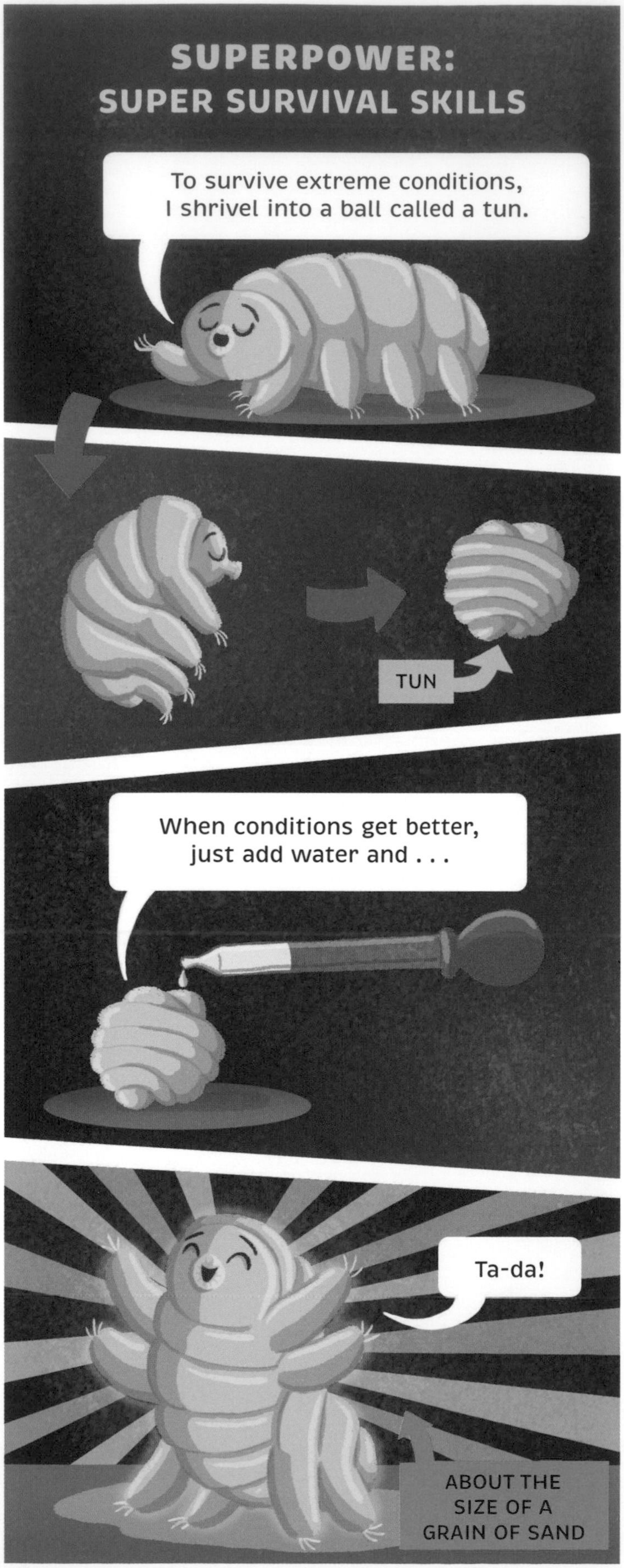
To survive extreme conditions, I shrivel into a ball called a tun.
TUN
When conditions get better, just add water and . . .
Ta-da!
ABOUT THE SIZE OF A GRAIN OF SAND

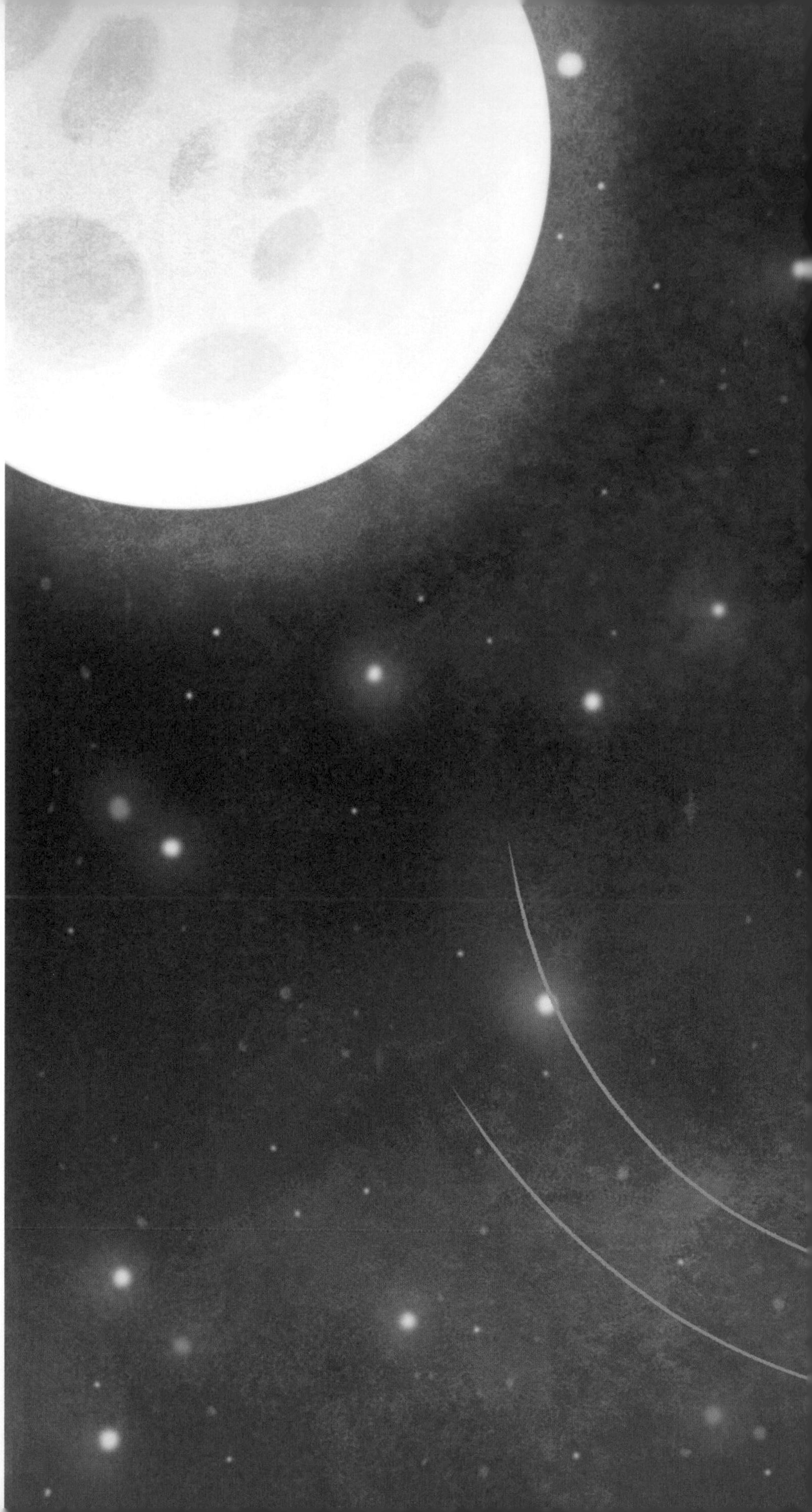

Tardigrade

The tardigrade, or water bear,
is so small that it's barely there.
Yet like big bears, it bears sharp claws—
on all *eight* of its tiny paws.
And bear in mind, although it's wee,
it's tougher than you'll *ever* be.
Freezing cold or boiling hot—
too much to bear? This bear thinks not.
Thirty years without a meal?
The tardigrade says no big deal.
Radiation? Outer space?
A nice relaxing change of pace.
So grizzly, polar, black bear too,
your trio's tough. *Grrrr*, here's to you.
But toughest *ursa* anywhere?
That prize goes to the water bear.

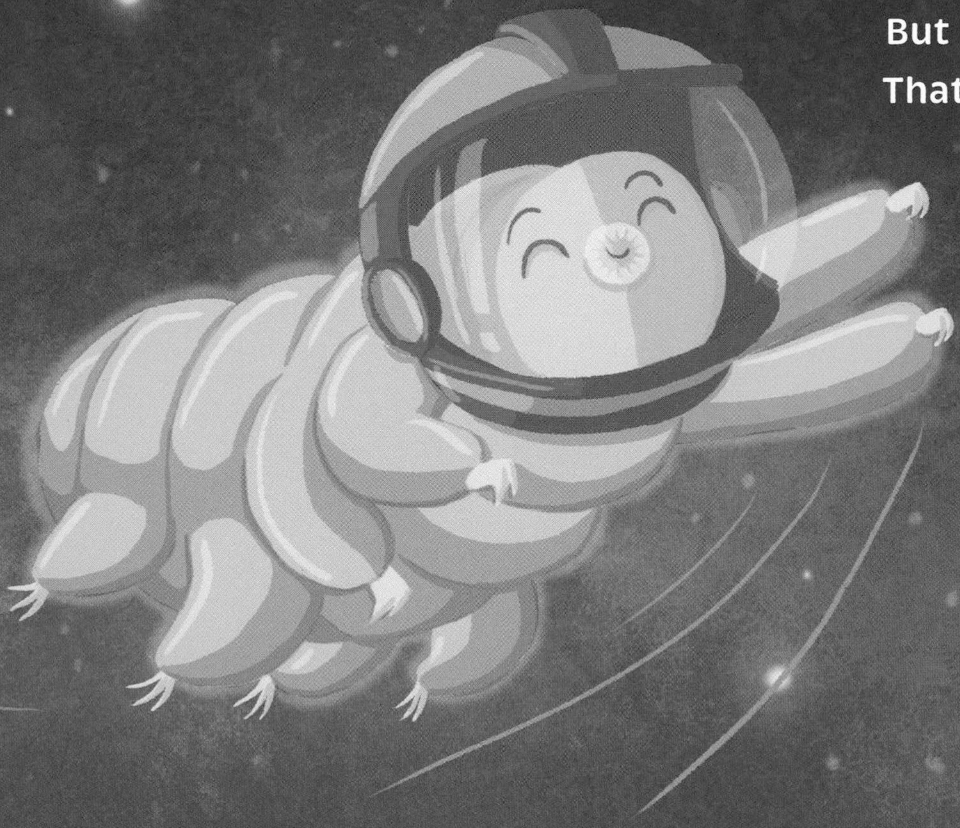

Barbados Threadsnake

Not a noodle,
not spaghetti,
angel hair,
or vermicelli.
Watch it wiggle
on its belly.
Hear it hiss,
politely tell me,
“Not a noodle.
Not sssspaghetti.
Little *ssssssssnake*.”
Extraordinary!

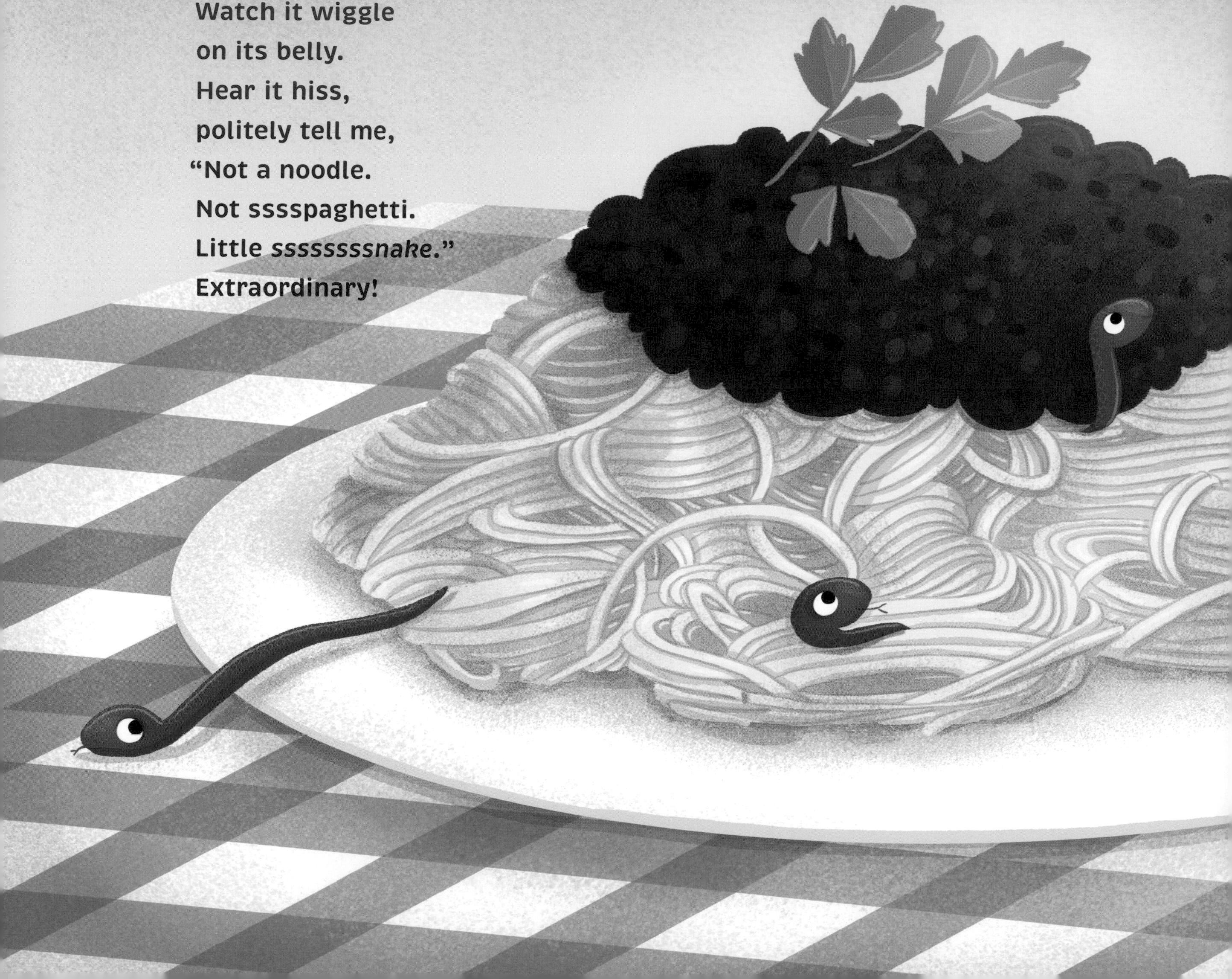

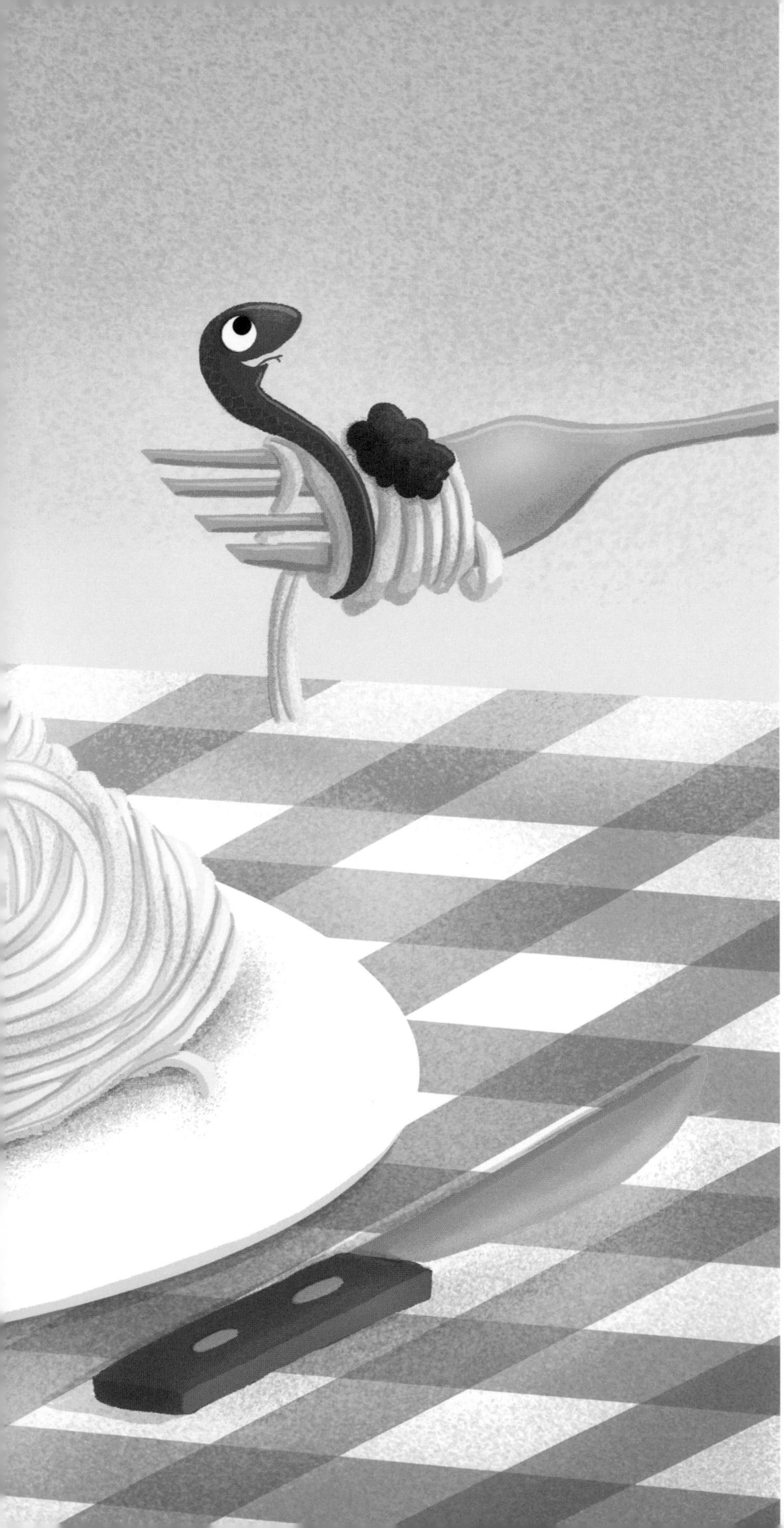

SUPERPOWER: SUPER SMALL SIZE

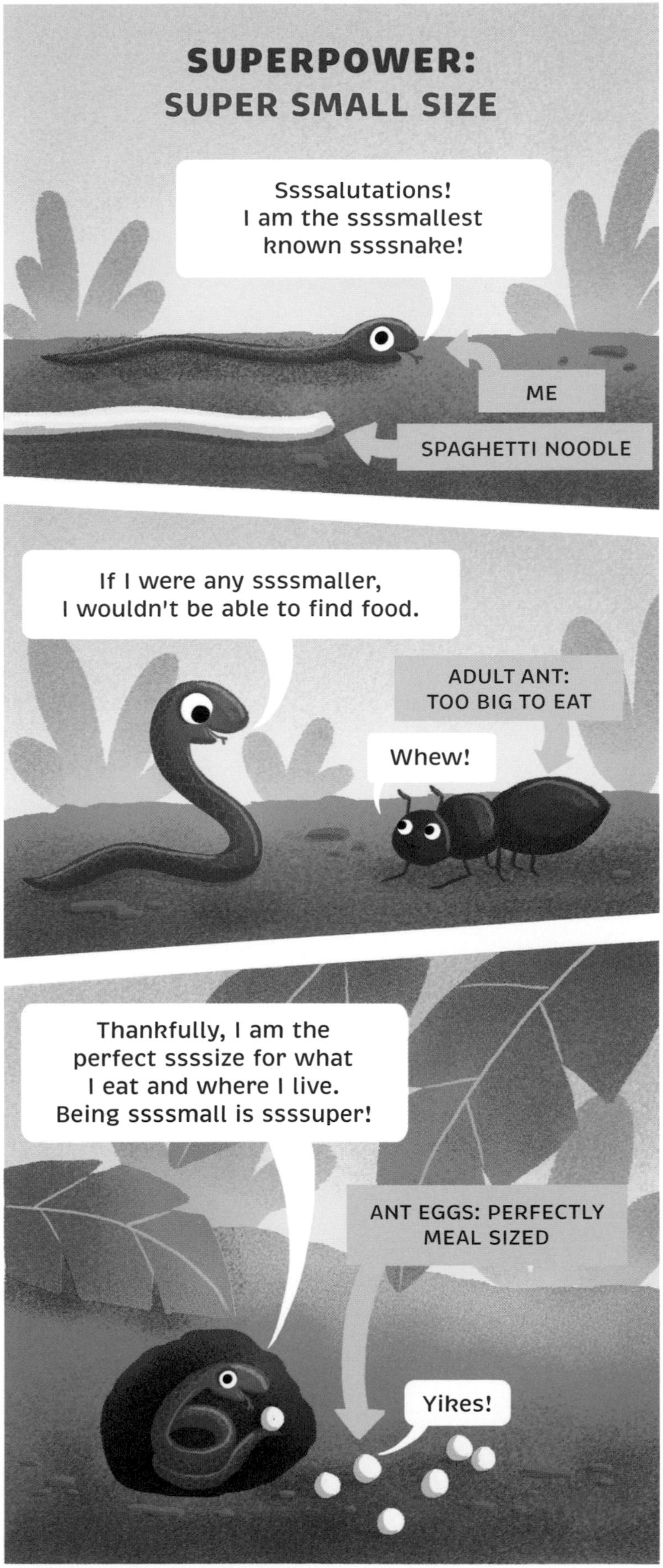

Ssssalutations! I am the sssssmallest known ssssnake!
ME
SPAGHETTI NOODLE
If I were any ssssmaller, I wouldn't be able to find food.
ADULT ANT: TOO BIG TO EAT
Whew!
Thankfully, I am the perfect ssssize for what I eat and where I live. Being ssssmall is ssssuper!
ANT EGGS: PERFECTLY MEAL SIZED
Yikes!

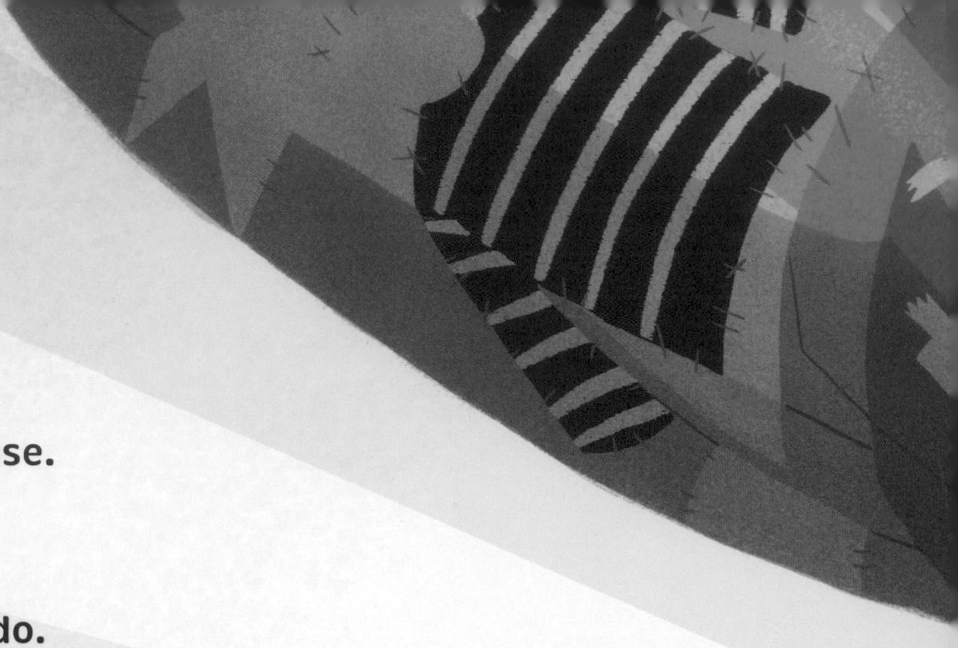

"You're just a kid," is their excuse.
"Too super small to be of use."
But I know this isn't true.
There's lots of stuff that I can do.
Because they think I'm only small,
they don't suspect a thing at all.
They'll be amazed at what I did—
even though I'm "just" a kid!

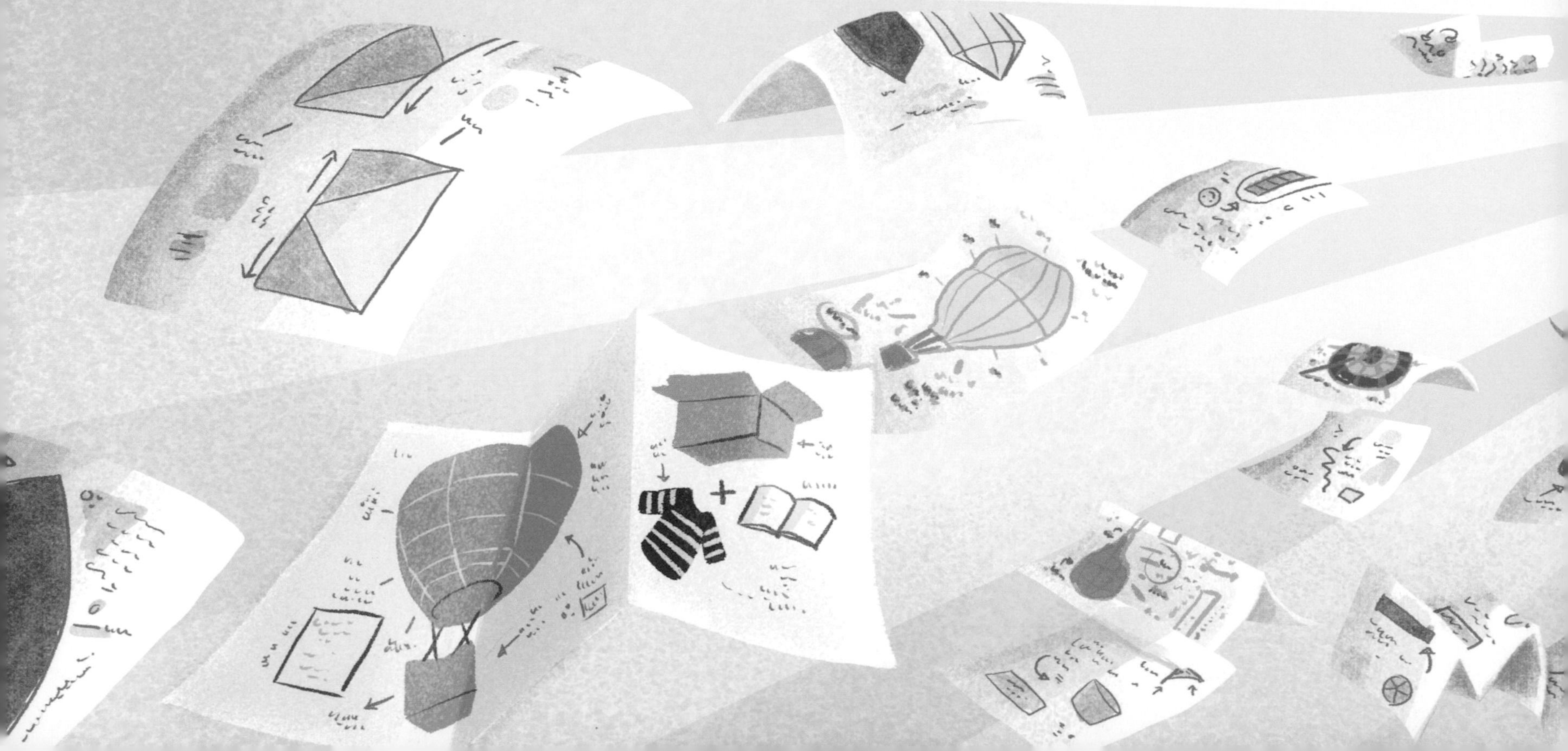

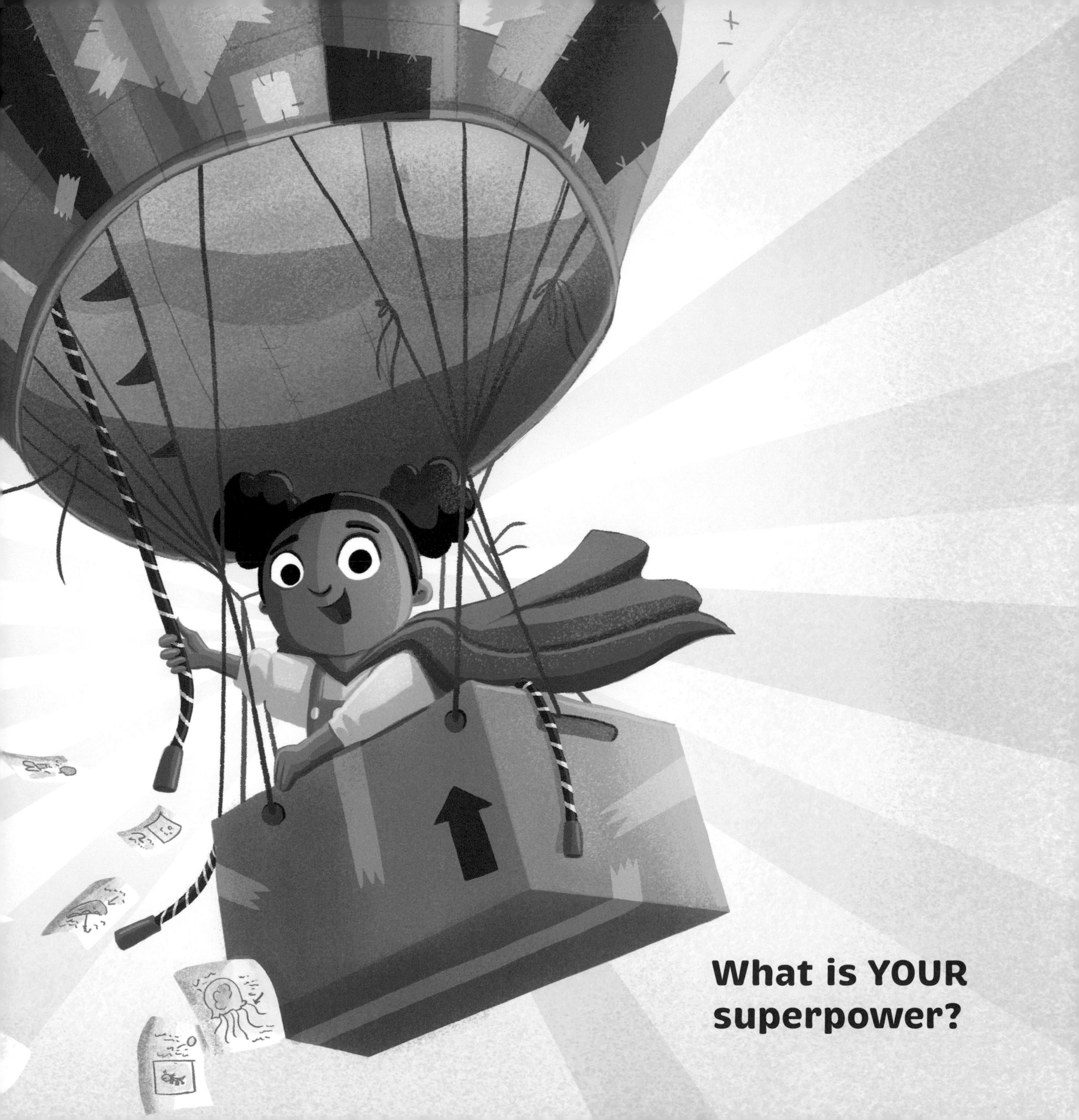

What is YOUR superpower?

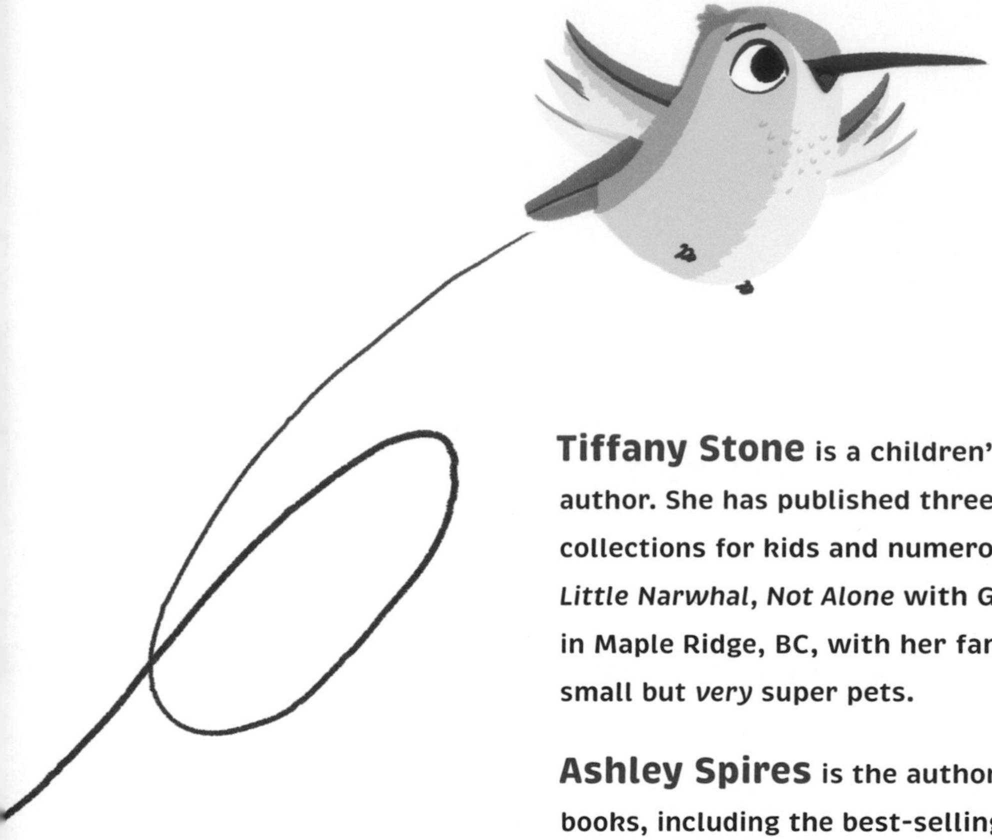

Tiffany Stone is a children's poet and picture book author. She has published three critically acclaimed poetry collections for kids and numerous picture books, including *Little Narwhal, Not Alone* with Greystone Kids. Tiffany lives in Maple Ridge, BC, with her family and several sort of small but *very* super pets.

Ashley Spires is the author and illustrator of many books, including the best-selling *The Most Magnificent Thing* and the Binky Adventure series, both of which have animated adaptations. When she is not making books, she enjoys yoga, jogging, and fostering orphan kittens for her local shelter. Ashley lives just outside Vancouver, BC, with her dog and far too many felines. Growing up, Ashley created teensy clay sculptures, some smaller than half your pinky fingernail!